Praise for

THE NEW TECH TITANS OF CHINA

You must read this book if you want to know where Chinese tech – from EVs to drones to robots to batteries to super-apps to e-commerce and all forms of AI – is headed in this era of cut-throat competition and poisonous geopolitics. Rebecca Fannin, with her singular insights and insider knowledge from decades of chronicling Chinese tech titans and their VC partners, takes the reader on a clear-eyed trek across today's perilous landscape where Chinese tech is besieged but also quickly catching up and sometimes surpassing global competitors.

Jim McGregor, Chairman, Greater China, APCO
Author, *One Billion Customers*

Rebecca Fannin has done something few western journalists have done – spend meaningful time with the Chinese entrepreneurs responsible for catalyzing China's innovation engine. She captures the spirit and struggles of being an entrepreneur in China as well as their extraordinary achievements.

Gary Rieschel, Founding Managing Partner, Qiming Venture Partners
Chair, Asia Society Northern California

Rebecca Fannin offers a sweeping, insider's view of China's evolving tech ecosystem—one that continues to surprise and outpace expectations. As someone who spent nearly two decades on the front lines at Alibaba, I find her new edition a valuable resource for business leaders seeking to understand the complexities and dynamism of China's innovation engine. Whether you're navigating global expansion or decoding market shifts, this book offers practical insight with real-world relevance.

Brian A. Wong, Author, *The Tao of Alibaba*

Rebecca Fannin's New Tech Titans of China is an important wakeup call for America and other advanced nations competing with China. Tech Titans clearly explains how China is accelerating ahead in technology leadership, and key technologies of the future including the Internet economy, AI, electric vehicles, drones and robots. Business leaders and policymakers need to read this book to understand the China tech challenge and what to do to not lose.

Dr. Robert D. Atkinson, President, Information Technology and Innovation Foundation

I met Rebecca back in early 2000's while chasing my American dotcom dream in Beijing. Her decades-long experience covering China technology sector gave her unique insights on the rise of Chinese technology industry. As China surpassing US in EVs, drones and robots and catching up on AI, the question remains—and I hope her next book will be about—what the best strategies are for US industrial and global talent policies to sustain US AI leadership.

Joe Chen, Chairman and CEO, Oak Pacific Investment
Founder, Renren, China's Facebook

Chinese tech titans are key actors on the world stage. Both China hawks and China doves need to understand companies like Alibaba, Baidu, and Tencent. Rebecca Fannin's book is a great place to start.

Isaac Stone Fish, Founder & CEO, Strategy Risks
Author, *America Second*

In the exhilarating age of drones, robots, and monumental tech innovation, Rebecca Fannin's book brilliantly chronicles the high-stakes showdown for tech leadership between the US and China, providing a quick, educational and compelling read.

John E. Oden, Principal & Co-Head of Family Offices, Asia, AllianceBerstein
Founder and Chairman Emeritus of the China-US Business Alliance

Few have chronicled the constant transformation of China's fast-moving tech world as long as Rebecca, and this timely update captures the most important shifts shaping its dynamic current chapter.

Rui Ma, China Tech Analyst
Creator, TechBuzz China

Rebecca's insights help one stretch their thinking and strategy deeper than ever possible without her dynamic points of view.

Purvi Gandhi, Managing Partner, Quain Investments

THE NEW TECH TITANS OF CHINA

Innovation Under Pressure in the World's Most Ambitious Economy

Rebecca A. Fannin

First published in Great Britain by John Murray Business in 2026
An imprint of John Murray Press

1

A CIP catalogue record for this title is available from the British Library

Trade Paperback ISBN 9781399810944
ebook ISBN 9781399826549

Typeset by KnowledgeWorks Global Ltd.

Printed and bound in the United States of America

John Murray Press policy is to use papers that are natural, renewable and recyclable products and made from wood grown in sustainable forests. The logging and manufacturing processes are expected to conform to the environmental regulations of the country of origin.

John Murray Press
Carmelite House
50 Victoria Embankment
London EC4Y 0DZ

John Murray Business
Hachette Book Group
123 South Broad Street
Ste 2750
Philadelphia, PA 19109, USA

www.johnmurraybusiness.com

John Murray Press, part of Hodder & Stoughton Limited
An Hachette UK company

The authorised representative in the EEA is Hachette Ireland, 8 Castlecourt Centre, Dublin 15, D15 XTP3, Ireland (email: info@hbgi.ie)

Dedicated to my family in two Fairfield counties of the USA

Contents

crackdown on their supersize. Today, they are regrouping and charging into artificial intelligence (AI) and investing multibillions in large language models (LLMs) to fuel future growth.

Chapter 3

Next-Gen Mobile Apps Leapfrog over PC Era 51

The next tier of Chinese tech leaders—TikTok owner ByteDance, Meituan, and Xiaomi—have leveraged China's vast mobile internet market to expand in China and are diversifying into entirely new fields and regions to spread their innovative skills more broadly.

Chapter 4

A Revolving Door Shuts on US–China Tech Deals 75

Dealmaking between the US and China is slowing down as geopolitical tensions intervene to nearly halt cross-border mergers, acquisitions and joint ventures, and curb investment in startups. This is just one aspect of decoupling.

PART TWO

Silicon Dragon-Style Venture Capital Gets Swept Up in Crosscurrents 89

Chapter 5

A Not-So-Golden Era for Cross-Pacific Venture Capital 91

Currents run strong across the Pacific to stop the flow of venture investments as Beijing and Washington exert more control. Once active cross-border venture capital (VC) firms such as Sequoia Capital and GGV Capital have been forced to make a choice between China and

the US. Many top venture capitalists have turned away from former hunting grounds in Chinese startup hubs and instead are scouting in Stanford and Berkeley or separately in Tsinghua and Fudan for the next new thing. This chapter also serves as a look at who's who among the leading venture investors in China, and how they have restructured in this new era.

PART THREE

An Exploration of China's Gain in the Tech Sectors That Matter Most 119

Chapter 6

A China–US Face-off in Artificial intelligence 121

China lags OpenAI in advanced artificial intelligence (AI) but is catching up quickly, as Hangzhou-based startup DeepSeek suddenly demonstrated. Chinese tech titans have also entered the fray with their own large language models.

Chapter 7

A Not-so Shared Economy 141

Startups in China's once-promising bike-sharing, coworking, and ride-hailing markets such as Mobike, Ucommune, and DiDi have slowed down in an overheated and highly regulated environment that saw some collapses like well-funded Ofo. Yet they showed the way for Lime, WeWork, and Uber.

Chapter 8

China's Dynamic Online Shops 155

Chinese e-commerce brands Temu and Shein have outpaced traditional e-retailers such as Alibaba and

Amazon with snazzy merchandising, duty-free goods, and social commerce but face new challenges such as tariffs in their pursuit of US sales.

Chapter 9

Chinese Electric Vehicle Makers Speed Past 169

China has accelerated into the electric vehicle (EV) market with few U-turns, led by strong contenders BYD and Xiaomi, with innovations and pricing that threaten to leave Tesla behind. The next battle will be over autonomous driving. Plus, a Q&A with autotech expert Michael Dunne who sounds the alarm for Detroit.

Chapter 10

The Age of Drones and Robots 189

Drones and robots are increasingly useful in factories, residences, military operations, and even in everyday life. Chinese makers like DJI and Unitree are putting their stamp on owning a substantial share of these fast-evolving markets. Humanoid robots are coming!

Afterword 207

The gap between the US and China is widening over technology leadership but not always with America ahead.

Acknowledgments 211
Notes 214
Index 238

INTRODUCTION

China's Silicon Valley has evolved over the past three decades as a dominant tech region that rivals the West. Once copiers and followers, Chinese tech entrepreneurs are charting their own future today and becoming less dependent on Western technologies.

In writing this new edition of *Tech Titans of China*, five years after the first, I knew there would be a lot to cover. What I didn't expect was the scale and speed of the changes.

To get back in the groove, I made a side trip from Hong Kong, where I was moderating at a tech and venture forum, to the southern Chinese city of Shenzhen, one of China's leading tech zones. The high-speed train across the border to Shenzhen was convenient and super quick, and within 30 minutes of leaving the Kowloon station, I'd arrived in in this bustling city that is home to Tencent, Huawei, BYD, and DJI. Soon I was on the local train, going to a startup hub to meet a manager of a tech accelerator and to hear what's new. With some directions from him, I got off at the right station but was soon lost in a sprawling, contemporary shopping mall, an exit nowhere in sight. A few people tried to help me by spotting the location on their mobile and showing me the screen. Through WeChat, I messaged my contact at the accelerator. As I told him landmarks I was walking by, he continued to text me along the way until I was outside and could spot him on the street just outside the entrance to his facility. Lucky!

I've traveled on my own in China most of the time, for 20 years, more than a hundred times. Returning now, I was caught up once again in the incredible energy of the street life in urban China—the buzz of China's fast-paced cities. The mopeds raced by, carrying deliveries, and I stepped aside to avoid being bumped. I missed my frequent stays, due to COVID-era lockdowns—and, I must add, the US–China geopolitical conflict.

Where there used to be collaboration, now the heated superpower race to lead tech has caused a split. China is more determined than ever to be the world leader in technology innovation—and the US is bullish about remaining number one. Cross-border US–China venture capital (VC) deals have evaporated and entrepreneurial and investment talent from the West have left once-vibrant tech hubs in Shanghai and Beijing.

Over the past two decades, China has transitioned from a fast follower of American ideas to an innovator on its own terms. Massive, multibillion-dollar efforts by the Chinese government seek to ensure that China catches up or leads in emerging technologies such as advanced artificial intelligence (AI). China is already ahead in high-speed rail, electric vehicles (EVs), robotaxis, digital payments, facial recognition, smart traffic control, drone deliveries, humanoid robots, and, yes, flying taxis. The clean and contemporary central business districts and airports of Shanghai, Beijing, and Hong Kong make New York City, Detroit, and Chicago centers look dated, or worse.

At the start of China's nascent tech economy, my up-close perspective covering the market and interviewing leaders gave me insights into a trend that Silicon Valley had largely ignored or dismissed, until now. I saw Chinese tech entrepreneurs working harder, innovating faster, and going global. I labeled China's evolving Silicon Valley–like startup culture as Silicon Dragon. But could they win the tech race globally?

These dragons competed with America's leaders—Baidu against Google, Alibaba against Amazon, and Tencent against Facebook. They won the Chinese market with startup smarts, sheer drive, and better understanding of the local market—plus support of a tech ecosystem where startups could be champions. Google and Facebook were blocked and censored in China—and still are.

China's techie contenders owned important swaths of an emerging tech economy in the world's most populous nation that was embracing private enterprise. An internet boom was like Silicon Valley during the dotcom rush of the late 1990s, except more intense. The US had its idols, and China had plenty of its own.

Despite the Chinese government crackdown on its tech giants, US restrictions on advanced technologies like Nvidia AI chips to China, and blocks on Silicon Valley investment in sensitive sectors such as quantum computing, China finds workarounds. Its inventiveness has continued to gain. Each pushback by the US has made China more determined to reach its goal of supremacy and self-sufficiency.

This is not to ignore the underlying problems in China's economy: high unemployment, slow growth, an aging population.

And in tech, the factors that keep it contained: increased state control over private enterprise and the US pushback on China's rise.

I know from experience that the entrepreneurial spirit of the Chinese people runs strong. The world's second-largest economy has a high-tech industrial policy, engineering talent, government subsidies, vast resources, scale, a strong supply chain, world-leading infrastructure, and ambition to become leaders in core technologies like robotics.

The US can no longer dismiss or ignore China's ascent. The Silicon Dragon has been awakened, and a new era of tech titans has arrived.

This book takes the reader on a journey to gain insights into the people, places, technologies, and capital that together show what's shaping this new superpower.

part one

HOW CHINA'S NEW ECONOMY KEEPS GAINING DESPITE CONSIDERABLE SETBACKS

CHAPTER 1

CHINA'S BID TO GET AHEAD IN TECH

A look in three sections at how the world's superpowers are caught up in a battle over chips, artificial intelligence (AI), and all the most important technology sectors globally. Five thought leaders sound off over the risks, barriers, and opportunities that will determine who wins this new tech race. Plus, a rundown, sector by sector, of major advances by China and how the US stacks up.

Section I: Overview

At the high-tech trade show Computex in Taipei, Jensen Huang, CEO of Nvidia, seemed to be everywhere wearing his signature leather jacket—on stage for a keynote, at a press conference, and surrounded by mobs of fans eager for his autograph. During a break, one young lady in the crowd brazenly approached him and asked Huang to sign her upper chest. That caught him off guard, and he hesitated momentarily, turning to the crowd—should I? Then he went ahead and signed, with a sly smile. The incident was picked up in a few social media posts and the local press, but soon more significant news stole the headlines in an ongoing US–China tech battle.

The energy and excitement at this Taiwan semiconductor conference that April surpassed any other trade show I've attended. One by one, Taiwan's leading chip CEOs took the stage to show off their latest products, and the crowd roared with approval. Jensen was their hero. He beamed, enjoying the attention that a chip CEO would never have enjoyed before US–China rivalry put integrated circuits into the middle of a feud.

A year later, at the same conference, CEO Huang struck a different tone. He called US export controls on chips to China a failure and said the restrictions have only pushed China to innovate faster. He fumed that Nvidia's market share in the country had dropped from 95 percent to 50 percent over the past four years. He pointed out Nvidia was missing out on sales to China after the US in April 2025 briefly restricted export of its H20 chip, which was developed specifically for the Chinese market to comply with US export restrictions of its more powerful chips.

After the US chip curbs on Nvidia, Huang traveled to Shanghai and met with the mayor to discuss plans to build an R&D center focused on Chinese markets for electric vehicles, autonomous driving, and data centers for cloud computing and AI. He also met with Chinese vice premier He Lifeng in Beijing to encourage more cooperation and explore how the American chip maker could maintain its foothold in China.[1] The tech world was paying attention as the US approved a restart of exports of its H20 chip to China, then Beijing put pressure on Chinese companies not to buy it due to data security concerns. How things would eventually pan out between the world's two biggest economies remained a big issue, but judging from past conflicts, China would increasingly seek to become self-reliant, as it's done with electric vehicles, AI, solar, and batteries.

High Stakes with Chips

Nowhere is this superpower tech rivalry more pronounced than in chips (not the flavorful kind), which power our iPhones, PCs, Teslas, data centers, missiles, and smart bombs.

Semiconductors were an American invention some 70 years ago. It was US technology and knowhow that helped launch Taiwan's semiconductor industry, transforming the island from a low-tech exporter into the world's chip-making powerhouse, with TSMC, founded in 1987 by pioneering chip technologist Morris Chang with Taiwanese government support. Today, Taiwan or Silicon Island makes 90 percent of the world's most advanced chips, supplying Apple and Nvidia from Hsinchu Science Park, a base for 500 companies and $363 billion in revenues – and a focal point for geopolitical tensions.[2]

Beijing's master plan, Made in China 2025, and the "Big Fund" of $145.5 billion have supported China's ambitious goal to become 70 percent self-sufficient in chip production and reduce reliance on imports.[3] It's worth noting that the US is investing heavily to bring back semiconductor production from Asia to American shores, (see Afterword).

China's efforts have centered on its home-grown chip plant, Semiconductor Manufacturing International Corporation (SMIC), founded in Shanghai in 2000 with $1 billion from a state-backed industrial group, domestic bank loans, and several international investors including Asia-Silicon Valley firms—Walden International and H&Q Asia Pacific—in addition to Goldman Sachs and Singapore's Vertex Management.

Early on in SMIC's development, I got a tour by then-CEO Richard Chang, a Taiwanese American engineer and former executive at Texas Instruments, who was recruited to lead the foundry located at Zhangjiang Hi-Tech Park in Shanghai's Pudong free trade zone. Wearing full cleanroom gear, he showed me the fab (semiconductor factory) and adjacent housing, even a church, for overseas engineers and their families. The area wasn't industrialized yet, and was mostly open fields, except for construction around the newly built Pudong International Airport.

In 2003, SMIC secured $630 million investment from two more prominent Silicon Valley firms, New Enterprise Associates (led by legendary venture capitalist Dick Kramlich[4]) and Oak Investment Partners, as well as Singaporean sovereign wealth fund Temasek. A year later, Motorola joined in through a swap of its underused Tianjin chip plant.

Pioneering private equity investors Ta-Lin Hsu[5] of H&Q Asia Pacific and Lip-Bu Tan of Walden International (now also CEO of Intel)—were at the forefront of the action. "The setting up of SMIC in Pudong was the first of some powerful pivotal moments for the Chinese chip industry and the dramatic rise that came after," Silicon Valley–based tech venture investor Purvi Gandhi recalled as together we reflected on these momentous times in China's push forward. She was on the investment committee of the H&QAP $750 million fund that initially backed SMIC.

By 2004, the Chinese chipmaker had gone public, raising $1.8 billion in New York City and Hong Kong. But leadership changes, operational struggles, legal battles over intellectual property, and limited profitability followed. In 2019, SMIC delisted from the New York Stock Exchange and then turned to Shanghai's Nasdaq-like STAR market, to pull in $7.6 billion. Subsequent funding led SMIC to effectively become a state-owned enterprise, a Silicon Valley venture advisor close to the transactions told me in a disheartened tone of voice.

Hampered by geopolitical tensions and curbs on access to advanced equipment to make high-end chips, SMIC lagged technology leaders Samsung in Korea and TSMC in Taiwan. While export restrictions have slowed China's bold goals for chip supremacy, that hasn't deterred its quest. With government support, SMIC, in 2023, broke through with making an advanced chip for new mobile phones by Huawei, which had been cut off from supplies by TSMC and Nvidia. Huawei plans to continue using SMIC-made chips for its smartphones. The Chinese telecom and tech conglomerate had just achieved its own major advance, building an operating system as an alternative to Google's Android and Apple iOS.

These made-in-China feats despite barriers and the heightened US–China tech conflict demonstrates once again China's strengthening bid for technology independence. In such important sectors, what happens here impacts the development of many other technologies globally.

Section II: The Big Picture with Five Experts

Through a series of interviews led by the author with technology innovation and investment leaders, we next delve into how China is continuing to forge ahead and compete with the US for leadership.

Gary Rieschel: Founding Managing Partner, Qiming Venture Partners and Chair, Asia Society Northern California, Seattle
Paul Triolo: Partner, China and Technology Policy Lead, DGA-Albright Stonebridge Group, Washington, DC
Ker Gibbs: Partner, Foresight Group / Executive-in-Residence, University of San Francisco / past president, American Chamber of Commerce in Shanghai, San Francisco
Isaac Stone Fish: Founder & CEO, Strategy Risks/ Visiting Fellow, Atlantic Council, New York City
Craig Allen: Senior Counselor, The Cohen Group/ Past President, US–China Business Council, Washington, DC
Rebecca A. Fannin: Author, *Tech Titans of China* (2019), *Silicon Heartland* (2023), *Startup Asia* (2011), *Silicon Dragon* (2008), Founder/Editor, Silicon Dragon Ventures, Contributor, CNBC and *Newsweek*

***Fannin:* How innovative are Chinese tech companies?**

Allen: China has already moved from being an innovation sponge to an innovation leader. The collective top priority of the central government is technology. Do not underestimate China's capabilities at engineering-based or science-based innovation.

Rieschel: The West has underestimated the sheer power of China's ability to take A to A prime, a one to a two, to a three. The Chinese are phenomenal at that.

Gibbs: The way Chinese innovate leans more towards the application and business model and leans less on the basic science. Take WeChat, for example. WeChat did not invent the mobile phone, electronic payments, or instant messaging. But it invented a business model that draws from all those capabilities. It's incredibly useful and convenient for millions of consumers.

Triolo: There are clear areas where the Chinese are way ahead, like in new energy vehicles and batteries. China is really pushing the envelope on humanoid robots too. And there's a little edge to China in smart devices from Xiaomi and Huawei, in designing both the hardware and software. Of course, there is also DeepSeek's progress in AI.

***Fannin:* Can, and will, China become self-reliant in technology?**

Rieschel: China will try to become as independent as possible. That's going to include semiconductors, manufacturing, AI and the application of AI, and it's going to include biotech.

Triolo: Huawei is at the center of a whole effort by the Chinese government to do more domestically, to help support the industry, to recreate large portions of the entire semiconductor supply chain. Huawei is being backed by the full faith and financing of the Chinese government.

Gibbs: China has capabilities to be self-sufficient in most areas, semiconductors being the glaring example to the contrary.

***Fannin:* How will China's techno-economy evolve?**

Rieschel: After Xi Jinping met with the 30 private company CEOs (in February 2025), SASAC, the group that manages state-owned enterprises, issued an edict to all the SOEs in China saying, you will implement AI technology based on DeepSeek or others as rapidly as possible. They've never done that before. What they're trying to do is re-host their entire enterprise software infrastructure now on AI. That's going to be powerful in putting up barriers for foreign firms.

If foreign firms aren't going to have any chance to compete, that's going to be a domestic (China) market. That's going to be huge.

Gibbs: We're in a transition phase right now. The famous meeting that Xi Jinping held with Chinese entrepreneurs, that was the olive branch. At the same time, the CCP [Chinese Communist Party] was offering them the opportunity to pledge to the Party and the plan. This group is very savvy, and they are going to be looking for some concrete measures about the ability to invest in and operate as more of a free market economy the way they did in the past. Is China going to be a centrally planned economy or is China going to go down the path that Deng Xiaoping established so many years ago – to give freer rein to the entrepreneurial spirit of the Chinese people? There are two different futures.

Fannin: **Will the current nationalistic protectionism approaches to technology work?**

Rieschel: Countries that have taken the position of trying to throw a moat around their technology and protect it have not been nearly as successful in history as those that did diffuse the technology and made it as broadly available as possible, effectively accelerating the adoption of the technology. If you look at the overriding policy considerations, such as the US trying to protect its technology, is that shortsighted? It will cause China to push harder at innovating on its own.

Fish: The geopolitical situation is hurting the Chinese tech industry. It's causing Beijing to be more paranoid than it would have been otherwise. Chinese tech entrepreneurs want to get out and don't want to be starting companies in China or keeping their assets in China.

***Fannin:* How will US supply chains shift given US–China trade issues?**

Rieschel: US firms are realizing that they were probably too concentrated on China. They're going to have to broaden their supply chain and lessen their dependence. Here's the trade-off. The Chinese supply chains have been incredibly efficient, better than virtually any other country in the world.

Because of geopolitics, companies are looking into other technologically developed places in Southeast Asia, more cooperation with Japan and Korea, and also into India, Brazil, and Argentina.

Triolo: China's manufacturing sector is so big and capable, and it's built for export, built to do advanced production at scale. The supply chains are all still largely in Asia—in Taiwan, Japan, Korea. Reversing four decades of manufacturing optimization in Asia for geopolitical reasons is really tricky. And it doesn't happen by magic or by government fiat. There has to be some commercial logic to it. Right now, a lot of what has been de-risked or moved out of China to Vietnam and Malaysia and other places has been done, but those countries have a limited capacity to absorb this.

Fish: There's a reason why companies are in China. It's efficient, it's relatively easy, and it's cheaper. India is making a lot of progress but there's still issues with bureaucracy, languages, and roads. It's not there yet, and whether or not it'll ever be the "quote, unquote" factory of the world is still an open question.

***Fannin:* How will decoupling of US and China tech ecosystems unfold?**

Gibbs: The Great Firewall is a very deliberate act to not couple, a completely different ecosystem in China and the rest of the world. Now they've gotten a deliberate push from the US to decouple. Decoupling is here to stay, and the question is, how complete will it be?

Fish: One of the biggest drivers of decoupling away from China has been the actions of the Chinese Communist Party and their pretty strong leftist turn over the last five years for pushing more state control of the economy. China is not as hospitable to entrepreneurship as it was even two or three years ago.

Triolo: The US premise is still being driven by this idea of slowing China's ability to develop advanced AI capabilities, to maintain US leadership and get to artificial super intelligence before China. That dynamic is not going away. It could upend the US–China relationship and create significant disruptions globally to supply chains, and cause conflicts over Taiwan or over AI's potential that could be dangerous.

Fannin: **How is the competitive landscape changing in the semiconductor industry?**

Gibbs: The industry is so global that it requires cross-border cooperation. There's been a lot of speculation about why China has done so well in batteries, solar, EVs, and yet semiconductors—despite the amount of capital China has put into the industry—it still seems unable to catch up.

Triolo: The vast majority of advanced semiconductors will continue to be manufactured on this little island Taiwan, within a narrow band on the west coast between Taipei and Tainan, and will be packaged there, too. So that's the reality. The numbers will come down with a little less dependence on Taiwan, but not significantly.

Section III: Signals of a Decided Tilt toward China Tech

This section, at a glance, defines how China is advancing on many fronts in the race for superpower status: tech foundations, resources, emerging sectors, venture investments, inventions, communications, talent, and wealth.

At its core, China's power base stems from deepening roots in industrial tech and AI that largely drives it. Meanwhile, the US continues to be a melting pot of new ideas and creativity, rooted in its culture. America's pioneering technology advancements, from the smart phone to generative AI, lead the world although China is gaining in applying new tech, from robotics to solar power to autonomous driving.

Foundations

Semiconductors

- China's "Big Fund" for major investment and the Made in China 2025 policy outlined semiconductors as one of 10 priority sectors to encourage indigenous innovation and tech leadership. China's chip industry is striving to become self-sufficient, boosted by heavy subsidies and engineering talent in spite of US pushback that has cut off its access to high-end chips from overseas.
- In 1990, the US produced 37 percent of chips globally but only 10 percent three decades later.[6]
- China is the biggest spender on chip-making equipment, $38 billion this year,[7] compared with $14 billion for the Americas, the fourth largest.

- While the US offshored much of its chip manufacturing to East Asia, America retained dominance in chip design, holding a 60 percent share of the so-called "fabless" semiconductor market, led by Nvidia, Intel, AMD, and Qualcomm.[8]

Manufacturing

- China is the world's factory with a massive supply chain while the US is struggling to rebuild its industrial production base.

Artificial Intelligence

- China is the global leader in patent applications for generative AI. China is launching innovative startups such as DeepSeek with more efficiency—and without VC funding.[12]
- Chinese tech titans Baidu, Alibaba, and Tencent are investing mega-billions in commercializing their own large language models, and are among the top 10 filers for generative AI patents.
- A breeding ground for GenAI startups is clustered around China's tech-centered Tsinghua University.
- China counts half the world's top AI researchers and leads in volume of AI research.

Resources

Rare Earth Minerals

- China controls 90 percent of the supply of rare earth minerals, used for making computers, TVs, and smartphones, as well as in many advanced defense weapons.

- As the US–China trade war intensified, China banned export of technologies for rare earth extraction and restricted export of the critical minerals, causing supply shortages for Detroit automakers. MP Materials, the only active US rare earth mine (in California near the Nevada border), has stopped shipments to China for processing, and plans to expand operations in Texas to boost supply.[13]

New Energy

- China has cemented its lead as the world's largest clean energy investor, as global investments hit a record $2.2 trillion. Over the past decade, China's share of global clean energy spending has risen from one-quarter to almost one-third, underpinned by investments in solar, wind, hydropower, nuclear, batteries, and electric vehicles (EVs).[14]
- Wind and solar account for 37 percent of China's power capacity, and are expected to surpass coal, which currently supplies 39 percent.[15]
- China produces 80 percent of the world's solar energy panels, while the US depends on imports from Southeast Asia and is seeking to reduce dependence on foreign suppliers.
- The US is retreating from clean energy initiatives for wind and solar projects under the Trump administration's policies.

Industrial Robots

- China leads the world in industrial robots, with a record 1.7 million at work, and gains of nearly 300,000 annually in Chinese electronics and automotive factories.

This represents 51 percent of the market, up from one-fifth 10 years ago.[16] The US counts 38,000 industrial robots.[17]

Humanoid Robots

- There are more than 160 humanoid robot makers worldwide, and China has the most—60—followed by Europe with 40 and the US with 30.[18]

Drones

- China leads the world in drone manufacturing and innovation. Chinese company DJI claims 70 percent of the overall drone market and 90 percent in consumer drones. China's EHang is advancing in flying drone taxis for passengers and plans to begin tests of commercial service in short distances.

Supercomputers

- The US is home to 5 of the 10 most powerful supercomputers in the world and has 173 of the leading systems worldwide, while China has 63 supercomputers. El Capitan, at Lawrence Livermore National Laboratory in California, is the world's most powerful.[19]

Quantum Computing

- China is claiming significant strides in quantum computing with major increases in speed and performance that surpasses classic supercomputers and Google's previous results.[20]

Sectors

Biotech

- China's recent breakthroughs in biotech have been described as a quiet DeepSeek moment for its gains from generics, growth in contract manufacturers, and emerging leaders in fast, cost-efficient drug discovery.[21] Chinese biopharmaceutical companies raised $3.3 billion across 155 deals in 2024, with more than one-third of the financing from US funds.[22]
- Pfizer recently invested $100 million for a stake in China's 3S Bio Inc. and sealed a $6 billion licensing agreement with the cancer treatment drug maker.
- Over the past 10 years, China's share of clinical trials rose from 3 percent in 2013 to 28 percent, while the number of China biotech licensing deals more than doubled to 33 in 2023,[23] mostly in oncology. Moreover, Chinese researchers published 60 percent of the world's most highly cited papers on synthetic biology in 2023, while US researchers accounted for just 7 percent—almost a flip from 2010, when the US held 45 percent of the most highly cited papers compared to China's 13 percent.[24]
- Venture capitalist *Rieschel on licensing:* "China has made great progress over the last decade in building out an innovative biotech and pharma ecosystem. The Pfizer's and Lilly's have multiple teams of people scouring China for opportunities to license Chinese healthcare and biotech technology, and bring it to the US. That's a big trend now compared to five years ago. It's orders of magnitude greater. The pharmaceutical industry in the last three years has invested $100 billion in licensing

Chinese biotech drugs and new pharma drugs—it's unprecedented."

- *Rieschel on regulations:* "The likelihood of US investment restrictions on Chinese biotech companies is a maybe. But the Chinese ecosystem is now at critical mass, so US government controls will not do much to slow down Chinese development."[25]

Genomics

- A scientist in China who was the first to create gene-edited babies in 2019 was jailed for three years and fined, but he is now back in the lab working on new research for treatment of diseases. His work had led to a controversy over demand for "designer babies."[26]
- The US retains leadership in genomics, although China is making rapid advances with several investment initiatives and extensive data collection.

Agritech

- China is progressing in agritech with the use of AI, aiming to boost production through an agricultural masterplan from the government.[27] It's using AI-driven drones and machinery to maximize crop yields and fill in a labor shortage in rural areas. Technology is getting embedded everywhere on farms, tracing where ingredients are sourced through the Internet of Things (IoT), using facial recognition to monitor the health of a pig, and placing sensors on legs of a chicken to check quality through monitoring how many steps it took.[28]

Transportation

Electric vehicles

- China is the world's electric car manufacturing hub, representing more than 70 percent of global production. Almost half of all car sales in China are electric, more than 14 million and climbing.[29] BYD recently surpassed Tesla in China sales while US manufacturers have struggled to compete in the Chinese market and face supply chain issues in Detroit.

Railways

- China boosts a vast high-speed rail network of nearly 30,000 miles connecting major cities across the country. The US has limited high-speed rail infrastructure. The Amtrak Acela service in the Northeast Corridor can reach high speeds only on certain segments of the line.[30]
- A Chinese railway manufacturer is testing China's first hydrogen-powered urban train that can reach 160 miles per hour and run for 190 hours—a milestone in green and low-carbon transportation.[31]

EV Charging Stations

- China has the most EV charging stations in the world, considerably more than half of the global total.[32] China is building out its charging infrastructure to keep pace with EV sales, and is also going big with ultrafast charging stations, for example Beijing's buildout of 1,000 ultrafast charging stations in 2025.[33] Additionally, the Chinese government is heavily supporting the idea of swapping depleted EV batteries for fully charged ones, with Chinese EV maker NIO the innovator and leader in China with more than 3,200 battery-swapping stations.[34]

EV Batteries

- China commands the EV battery market with a significant share while the US has fallen behind. Chinese EV battery maker CATL recently beat rival BYD's record with a fast-charging battery that can be driven 323 miles on a single charge of under five minutes.[35]

Shared Bicycles

- China spearheaded the development and expansion of dockless bike-sharing systems in the mid-2010s, although the craze led to several overstretched startup failures.[36] Shared bikes and scooters in the US are only a sliver of the scale in China.

Shipbuilding

- In only two decades, China has grown to be the dominant player in shipbuilding, claiming more than half of the world's commercial market, while the US share has fallen to next to nothing (just 0.1 percent).[37]

Spacetech

- China aims to break space technology choke points with thousands of experiments on the Tiangong space station over the next decade or so.[38]
- China became the first country to land on the far side of the moon, in 2019.

- The US was the first nation to land humans on the moon, with astronaut Neil Armstrong's famous step in 1969.

Investment

Venture Capital

- China VC investments climbed to $105 billion at the peak in 2018, almost surpassing the US. Since then, the gap has widened, with China at just $36.9 billion compared to the North American market, dominated by the US, with more than half of $397 billion in total global investment.[39] This seismic shift was caused by a series of dramatic changes: Chinese government crack-downs, an increase in state-led funds, and a geopolitical rift that led Sand Hill Road investors to back away.
- China plans to establish a $137 billion state-backed venture fund focused on investing over 20 years in high-tech industries including robotics.[40]

Venture Capitalists

- China venture capitalists have ranked high among the world's most successful investors several times, claiming 14 spots currently (a record 21 in 2019) on the *Forbes* Top 100 ranking.[41] Neil Shen, a former steward of Sequoia Capital who is now leading the separated China firm HongShan or HSG, has made the list 13 times, and he topped it four times.
- The US consistently takes a majority of the top 100 spots with venture capitalists Reid Hoffman, Peter Thiel, and Vinod Khosla as high scorers, and Sequoia's Alfred Lin ranked first now with an investment in OpenAI.

Unicorns and Decacorns

- The US leads the world for unicorns (privately held companies with valuations of more than $1 billion). Out of more than 1,200 unicorns globally, the US weighs in with 702 while China maintains a second position, counting 302 unicorns.[42] Five Chinese cities rank among the top 10 worldwide for unicorn count.[43]
- Of startups most likely to become gazelles—or "go unicorn" within three years—the US retained the top spot with 330, followed by China with 258.[44]
- TikTok owner ByteDance placed second worldwide as most valuable unicorn, recently overtaken by SpaceX.[45]
- China has more than a dozen decacorns (valued at more than $10 billion), led by TikTok maker ByteDance.[46] The US has 34 decacorns, with SpaceX top of the list.

Inventions

Patent Applications

- China surpassed the US for number of international patent applications in 2019, the first time that the US was not in the lead, and since then, China has maintained the top spot.
- China had 25.6 percent of 273,900 filings in 2024, dwarfing the US at 19.7 percent (and Japan at 17.7 percent).[47]
- China's telecom conglomerate Huawei Technologies has ranked first worldwide for patent applications for 10 consecutive years, filing for 6,000 in 2024. Samsung, Qualcomm, and Mitsubishi also place high.

Patents in Use

- China leads the world in number of active patents, with approximately 5 million. The US is second, with 3.5 million.[48]

Research and Development

- The US has outpaced the world in R&D spending in the past for scientific innovation, but China's pot is increasing faster—up 8.9 percent contrasted with 4.7 percent for the US. China investment in R&D reached $781 billion in 2023, compared to the US at $823 billion.
- In light of recent cuts in federal science spending under the Trump administration, China could overtake the US in this critical measure of competitiveness.[49]

Communications

Mobile Operating Systems

- China's telecom giant Huawei launched its own mobile operating system, HarmonyOS, on a new high-end smartphone in 2023,[50] marking a major step in the country's tech resilience despite efforts by Washington to restrict access to US chip-making knowhow. China is adopting HarmonyOS, creating a third global mobile operating system alongside Android and Apple iOS, with Huawei potentially exporting the system abroad.
- Next, Huawei is gearing up to test the technical capabilities of a new higher-end chip that could be a substitute for Nvidia's most advanced chip, restricted from exporting to China.[51]

6G

- China claims the world's first field tests of networks for 6G communication and, by 2030, aims to commercialize the improved technology for mobile phones.[52] China's Huawei is poised to lead this next generation of networking. Today, 45 percent of US mobile users are covered by 5G, compared with 88 percent of Chinese mobile users.[53]

Internet Users

- China has the highest number of internet users globally, at more than 1.09 billion, but its internet penetration rate of 78 percent[54] is lower than the US, where nearly everyone is online.[55]

Smartphone Users

- China smartphone adoption has grown rapidly to surpass 900 million users,[56] compared with 270 million for the US, where about nine in ten people now own a smartphone.[57]

Mobile Payments

- China is a cashless society through widespread adoption of digital wallets and QR-code transactions. Alibaba's Alipay and Tencent's WeChat Pay control more than 90 percent of digital payments in China. It's as if Amazon and Facebook were the major conduits for payments in the US (but aren't).[58]

Super Apps

- China pioneered super apps combining payments, e-commerce, and messaging such as WeChat, which today is used regularly by 1.2 billion in China. Facebook adapted WeChat's concept of a multi-functional app.

Livestreaming

- China was an early adopter of livestreaming[59] as well as social commerce, and both markets are significantly larger in China than in the US, propped by a strong mobile payment system, a large social media base, and popular brands.

Talent

Universities

- While the US has the most universities in the top 100 ranking by *US News & World Report*, Tsinghua and Peking Universities regularly feature on the list. China claimed 13 (including four from Hong Kong) of the top 100, compared to 41 from the US.[60]

Engineers

- In 2020, engineering comprised 33 percent of all first university degrees in China, as opposed to just 9 percent in the US. China awarded the most science and engineering doctorate degrees globally in 2020 (43,000), closely followed by the US (42,000).[61]

Architecture

- The winner of the Pritzker Architecture Prize in 2025 is Liu Jiakin for a commercial complex that fills an entire block with shops, bike paths, and walkways in his hometown of Chengdu.[62] In 2012, Wang Shu was the first Chinese citizen to win the prize, for a history museum in Ningbo that included locally recycled materials. Nine Americans have received the prize.

Nobel Prizes

- The US leads the world, by far, for the most Nobel Prize winners (423), awarded in several fields: physics, chemistry, medicine, and economic sciences. China ranks 22nd globally with eight awards given to Chinese nationals, three of them for physics.[63]

Wealth

Billionaires

- The US has the most billionaires (902) followed by China with 450,[64] up from 406 in 2024 but still short of its high point 495 in 2023. China's troubled property sector and turmoil in the country's financial markets are partly the cause.

Tech Billionaires

- The US leads globally with the most tech billionaires (Elon Musk, Mark Zuckerberg, Jeff Bezos, Larry Ellison, and Google cofounders Larry Page and Sergey Brin) while China ranks second with Pony Ma of Tencent, Zhang Yiming of ByteDance, Colin Huang of PDD / Temu, Jack Ma of Alibaba, Wang Chuanfu of BYD, and Lei Jun of Xiaomi.[65]

Silicon Valley Exceptionalism

- Nvidia surpassed Apple as the world's most valuable public company by market capitalization.[66]

- SpaceX is the world's most valuable private company, with a valuation of more than $350 billion.[67]
- OpenAI was founded in 2015 by Silicon Valley tech leaders and benefited from top-tier AI research talent, vast funding, and plentiful computing resources in the Bay Area.
- Elon Musk's Neuralink brain-implant company recently raised fresh capital at a $9 billion valuation, more than double its previous amount.
- Finally, and conclusively, Silicon Valley remains the world's leading tech innovation and venture capital center. The Bay Area continues to be a magnet for top talent, startups and breakthroughs, and commands a lead in AI.

CHAPTER 2

CHINA'S BAT STAY IN POWER

China's mighty tech titans—Baidu, Alibaba, and Tencent—have staying power in search, commerce, and social media despite the Chinese governmental crackdown on their supersize. Today, they are regrouping and charging into artificial intelligence (AI) and investing multibillions in large language models (LLMs) to fuel future growth.

China's tech giants have entered a bold new chapter. Once fueled by breakneck growth, global ambition, and relentless copying, Baidu, Alibaba, and Tencent—collectively known as BAT—rose to dominate by getting bigger, faster.

The BAT trio ruled China's digital core—search, shopping, and social. Then came a second wave: the "TMD" group—Toutiao (an engine behind TikTok), Meituan (China's lifestyle super app), Didi (its ride-hailing titan), and Xiaomi, the smartphone disruptor. Each one reshaped daily life in China for over a billion people and set its sights abroad.

A third wave surged forward—led by ultrafast fashion leader Shein, social commerce upstart Xiaohongshu ("Little Red Book"—known in the West as RedNote), and a swarm of innovators in electric vehicles, robotics, drones, and AI. In a single generation, China flipped the script: from copycat to contender, challenging the West on its own technological turf.

Then, poof! China's tech titans, the homegrown equivalents of Google, Amazon, and Meta, were abruptly cut down to size. Geopolitical tensions with the United States, tightening government oversight, and new barriers to cross-border investment and innovation all converged to halt their momentum. Baidu, Alibaba, Tencent, and others found themselves under intense scrutiny, with regulators in Beijing slashing monopolistic practices, targeting outspoken founders, and blocking initial public offerings (IPOs) deemed too risky. In response, China's tech titans sold off noncore assets, scaled back international ambitions, stopped investments in US tech startups, and turned their focus inward. The bold vision of "China for the World" gave way to a more insular "China for China" approach.

The era of freewheeling tech entrepreneurship transitioned to one defined by nationalism and strict state control. Foreign investors pulled back, wary of the regulatory environment and the growing tension between Beijing and Washington. A new generation of entrepreneurs emerged—more cautious and more in line with the machinery of the state.

But then, in early 2025, a ray of light shone through. Chinese President Xi Jinping held a gathering of the nation's tech champions. Seated prominently in the first row was Jack Ma, China's most famous internet entrepreneur who had avoided the spotlight for several years after a crackdown on Alibaba. His presence alone was a reassuring sign of a reopening of the stage for private sector visionaries. Xi asked for their help in growing China's economy and achieving greater self-reliance. The founder of AI innovator DeepSeek, whose models were touted as a viable alternative to Open AI, was symbolically front and center (see Chapter 6).

The event was seen as a confidence booster for the weakened private sector struggling with sluggish domestic demand and economic malaise. It signaled a new compact between the state and private enterprise. Innovation and growth aligned with national priorities would be supported in strategically vital sectors: AI, quantum computing, and chip manufacturing.

Silicon Valley be Damned

Today, China's tech titans are regrouping and plotting investments for a new era of strategic competition. The bruising trade tension with the US and an ongoing trade standoff have forced a sharper determination among Chinese tech leaders to chart their own path in both software and hardware. The message is unmistakable: China will build without or without Silicon Valley.

Despite the regulatory headwinds and geopolitical friction, these firms remain deeply entrenched in China's digital economy. Baidu continues to lead in AI-driven search and autonomous driving, Alibaba commands e-commerce and cloud computing, and Tencent dominates in social platforms and online entertainment. While they've had to move more cautiously, innovation hasn't slowed. If anything, it's become more focused. Each company is channeling capital and talent into frontier tech: generative AI, semiconductors, and smart devices. In a striking move, Alibaba recently struck a deal to embed its AI models into Apple iPhones sold in China.

Attuned to shareholders, growth objectives, and the spark lit by OpenAI in the US, China's tech giants are now developing advanced AI as a foundation to build out their businesses. Machine learning, facial recognition, and LLMs are being woven into industries from finance and e-commerce to logistics, smart manufacturing, and robotics.

DeepSeek's recent breakthrough showed China isn't merely catching up in AI. It's starting to lead in efficiency and performance, underscoring China's growing self-sufficiency. Billions in capital are being funneled into this AI surge. The BAT trio—Baidu, Alibaba, and Tencent—see generative AI as a transformative force on par with Edison's light bulb. Like Microsoft and Amazon that have backed OpenAI and Anthropic in the US, China's tech titans are strategically placing their own bets on homegrown startups such as Moonshot AI.

The fiercest contender may not be one of the BAT. ByteDance, parent of TikTok, is outspending the traditional tech titans (see Chapter 3).

The New Killer App in the Age of AI

Baidu broke ground in China's AI race in 2023, becoming the first major Chinese tech company to roll out an LLM. Just as global interest in generative AI surged, it launched ERNIE Bot—China's answer to OpenAI's ChatGPT, which remains inaccessible in China. Since then, Baidu has rapidly upgraded ERNIE, sharpening its language skills, memory, reasoning, and even emotional nuance like satire. Additionally, Baidu set up a $145 million fund to back Chinese AI startups. By moving early, Baidu is supercharging its core products and expanding into AI-driven ventures like autonomous driving and the

Apollo Go robotaxi fleet. CEO Robin Li sees generative AI as a game changer, predicting it will turn Baidu's search engine into the "killer app in the age of AI."

Alibaba is also making a big bet. It's pouring $52 billion over three years into AI and cloud computing, backing leading Chinese AI startups, and bundling its in-house model, Tongyi Qianwen, across e-commerce, digital marketing, and workplace tools for small businesses. Chairman Joe Tsai calls AI the company's engine of the future, reigniting its "startup passion and imagination."[1]

Not to be outdone, Tencent has tripled capital spending to $10.7 billion, zeroing in on AI as a top priority. The company has restructured internal AI teams to speed up product development and innovation while ramping up investment in its *Hunyuan* model suite, launched in late 2023 and boasting advanced tools such as text-to-video generation. Tencent is weaving Hunyuan into search, summary, and data analysis features for its flagship messaging app WeChat and video conferencing platform Tencent Meetings.

For China's tech titans, this AI moment isn't just an opportunity—it's an ultimatum. The race is on to reinvent themselves, building smarter, AI-native businesses that were not on the radar a decade ago. Baidu, Alibaba, and Tencent are moving fast, betting their futures on transforming how people communicate, shop, and travel—all powered by AI.

China's BAT Regroups

It wasn't long ago, around the turn of the century, that China's first generation of internet entrepreneurs were just getting started: Baidu's Robin Li, Alibaba's Jack Ma, and Tencent's Pony

Table 2.1

How China's BAT revenues grew

Company	2015	2020	2024	Forecast growth
Baidu	$10.16 B*	$16.41 B	$18.24 B	+3.1%
Alibaba	$12.29 B	$71.99 B	$130.35 B	+5.95%
Tencent	$15.81 B	$73.91 B	$95.65 B	+10%

*B = billion

Source: Company financial statements and annual reports

Ma. Silicon Valley skeptics largely dismissed them as copiers of Western knowhow, hardly a threat. Few imagined they would have come so far, so quickly—and stay in power for so long (see Table 2.1).

Nonetheless, the BAT companies broke through in China's digital economy, progressing from copying American leaders. They gained confidence and began to innovate, and—despite setbacks—began to create and adopt technologies ahead of the West. They were the first generation of tech entrepreneurs since the reforms of former leader Deng Xiaoping opened China to a socialist market economy and made it glorious to get rich.

The Chinese techno-preneurs became very rich, among the richest in the world—initially by replicating tech innovations from Silicon Valley. The new trend became to copy business models *from* Beijing, Shanghai, and Hangzhou. Notably, Facebook became more like Tencent's multifunctional WeChat.[2] TikTok inspired Reels.

China's challengers got venture capital from Sand Hill Road and international investors eager to tap into this new hotspot. The BAT grew revenues superfast in their home market, diversified, and expanded with investments in Southeast Asia and US tech hotspots. For nearly two decades—2000 to 2018—these titans seemed unstoppable. But the Silicon Dragon companies grew too fast and too far just as the climate for big tech was shifting in China. Their supersized monopolies were restructured and downsized, and they lost momentum.

This hit them on Wall Street. The market capitalizations of Baidu, Alibaba, and Tencent dropped from a peak in 2020 and 2021. Previously in the top 10 rankings by market cap, Alibaba and Tencent dropped out, displaced by Nvidia, Broadcom, TSMC, and others in the AI and chip-making era (see Table 2.2).

Table 2.2

Top 10 tech companies by market valuation: 2015/2025

Rank	**2015**	**Market cap (approx.)**	**2025**	**Market cap (approx.)**
1	Apple	$672–725 B*	Apple	$2.86 T*
2	Google	$497 B	Microsoft	$2.83 T
3	Microsoft	$426 B	NVIDIA	$2.47 T
4	Facebook	$295 B	Amazon	$2.28 T
5	Amazon	$294 B	Alphabet (Google)	$1.82 T
6	**Tencent**	$200–250 B	Meta (Facebook)	$1.13 T
7	**Alibaba**	$200–220 B	Tesla	$1.10 T
8	Samsung	$200 B+	Broadcom	$1.08 T
9	Intel	$140 B	TSMC	$997 B
10	IBM	$150 B	Oracle *(fluctuating with TSMC)*	$350–400 B

*B = billion; T = trillion

Source: S&P Global Market Intelligence, Statista, *Forbes*

Table 2.3

How revenue and growth compare for Chinese and US tech giants

Company	2020 revenue	2024 revenue	1-year growth (2023–24)	4-year growth (2020–24)
Baidu	$16.4 B*	$18.2 B	–1%	+11%
Alibaba	$72.0 B	$130.0 B	+8%	+81%
Tencent	$70.0 B	$91.3 B	+11%	+30%
Alphabet (Google)	$182.5 B	$350.0 B	+13.6%	+92%
Amazon	$386.1 B	$574.8 B	+11.8%	+49%
Meta (Facebook)	$86.0 billion	$116.6 B	+19.7%	+36%

*B = billion

Source: Company annual reports, industry analyses, and financial news sources

Longtime US–China venture capitalist Gary Rieschel observed that China's BAT were among the most valuable publicly traded companies worldwide in 2014. "Now the top 10 Chinese tech companies don't even come close to one of the US companies—Google, Apple, Amazon, Meta, Nvidia. They all just blew past Chinese counterparts," said Rieschel, who launched leading VC firm Qiming Venture Partners, an investor in numerous China tech startups.

Moreover, the growth rate of the Chinese tech titans was outpaced by the American leaders (see Table 2.3).

Boxing Their Way Out

Back in the day, the founders of China's BAT companies were iconic figures, looked up to like Steve Jobs of Apple was.

Emboldened, they supersized into powerful Chinese tech conglomerates by 2018 that paralleled Alphabet, Amazon, and Facebook for scope and influence. They diversified across finance, ridesharing, education, healthcare, and more within their home country, and then overseas. Tencent began trading on the Hong Kong Stock Exchange in 2004, then Baidu on Nasdaq in 2005 and Alibaba on the New York Stock Exchange in 2014.

Billionaires from their tech startups, China's BAT founders still play a dominant, strategic role. They have held on to their market-leading positions despite aggressive entrants that threaten their stronghold.

Quiet-spoken and determined, search expert Li paralleled Google with his first startup, Baidu (pronounced Buy-Do), and he won the Chinese market with a local understanding of the language and culture. Baidu surpassed Google in China to own 70 percent of the market and—with Google not searchable within China—claim approximately 544 million monthly users.[3] Alibaba's dynamic founder, Ma, modeled his Taobao shopping site after eBay and beat the online auction site in China with heavy discounts and an escrow-type payment method. Today, Taobao and its merchant's storefront, Tmall, are among the world's largest digital retail businesses, with 800 million users.[4] Tencent's often-elusive CEO, Ma Huateng (known as Pony Ma, derived from his family name, which means "horse" in China) developed the QQ instant messaging site in 1999 based on the Israeli invention ICQ, and in 2011, created the multifunctional super app WeChat, today used by just about everyone in China for messages, online shopping, and payments.

But there's always something new in China's online world. Today, short-form video app Douyin, the TikTok of China, is

Table 2.4

Chinese social media platforms: new rivals to BAT

Platform	2020	2025	Growth (%)
WeChat	1,225	1,400	+2.7%
Douyin	530	766	+7.8%
Tencent QQ	595	597	0%
Kuaishou	355	714	+ 9%
Weibo	550	582	+1.4%
Xiaohongshu	138	300	+ 16%
Total users*	3,363	4,095	+4.0%

* User figures in millions

Source: Industry reports, Statista, media coverage, annual reports; estimates based on compound annual growth rates.

the go-to place for online entertainment and social commerce. Little Red Book, or RedNote as it's commonly called, makes Instagram look stale with its feature-rich shopping and sharing. Video sharing and livestreaming app Kuaishou has moved into commerce. Pinduoduo's social shopping with group buying at discounts threatens Alibaba's lead (see Table 2.4).

What Excites Search Pro Li

Baidu cofounder Robin Li (b. 1968) was a novice entrepreneur born in a poor inland China city who got into computers at an early age and majored in library science at the prestigious Peking University. Eager to come to the US for graduate school, he sent out applications and got a fellowship at SUNY Buffalo. He earned a master's degree in computer science, concentrating on information retrieval, the roots of search, and later obtained a patent for ranking websites by hyperlinks. After a software job at a Dow Jones subsidiary and a project to create an online edition of *The Wall Street Journal*, he moved to Silicon Valley to work on an internet search engine for Infoseek. He was so immersed in Silicon Valley culture that he penned a book about the early dot-com battles and interviewed many Valley legends such as John Chambers and Steve Jurvetson. When Disney acquired Infoseek in 1999 and sidelined his project, Li decided to return home to China—like the many so-called sea turtles, or *haigui*, Chinese nationals returning after studies abroad to exploit the new opportunities in their homeland.

At about the same time that Google cofounders Larry Page and Sergey Brin were working on technology for searching the web, Li and his cofounder, Eric Xu, were fiddling with the same. Baidu, which translates as "seek for truth," a persistent search for the ideal, opened in January 2000 and, after several tries at a workable business model, took a hint from Google and plunged into the moneymaking model the American startup had used the year before: paid search from online advertisers. Tapping his connections, Baidu raised venture funds from Draper affiliate DFJ ePlanet. Li homed in on search technologies, his passion. He outdid Google in China with speedier and more reliable searches in Mandarin.

Looking to the future, he set up a Baidu R&D lab in Silicon Valley in 2014 to conduct AI research, primarily in self-driving software. He made a splash by appointing globally recognized deep learning pro and former Google Brain founder Andrew Ng as chief scientist of Baidu's 1,300-person AI group. The serious-minded and determined Li also ventured into other fields, for example a joint venture for new energy vehicles with Chinese automaker Geely and the acquisition of a controlling share in iQIYI, China's Netflix.

While appearing shy and reserved, Li had his sights boldly set across the Pacific, too. At the Consumer Electronics Show in Las Vegas in 2018, Baidu staged a flashy, coming-out party for a new line of AI-powered lights, speakers, and projectors. Chief operating officer Lu Qi, who had been hired from Microsoft, showed off the company's AI technologies and boasted that Baidu was "innovating at China speed," or superfast. He not so subtly dubbed this product line "the Alexa of China."

Like other Chinese tech giants hungry for more, Baidu was targeted by authorities. The search giant was warned that its app and browser were collecting more user data than necessary. Under a new cybersecurity law, watchdogs fined Baidu—as well as Tencent—for not doing enough to prevent pornography and violent content. Baidu and other China tech titans were also fined for violating antimonopoly legislation and failing to report past deals.

Some 25 years after starting Baidu, Li has stamina. He is totally into AI and remains firmly in charge as chairman and CEO. Baidu has faced headwinds and has not grown as fast as other titans, but it's no lightweight.

Alibaba Opens Doors

Alibaba owes much of its universal recognition to its founder. Jack Ma (b. 1964), in his mid-fifties, famously said he was too old to run an internet company and turned over the reins. He remains highly influential though not so visible. Alibaba's identity stems from its name, which conjures up the recognizable command Open Sesame, used by the fictional character Ali Baba to enter his cave full of treasures. Hardly press shy and with his gift for gab—in perfect English—Ma became known around the world.

A former schoolteacher in China, he practiced his English skills as a young boy while showing foreign tourists around Hangzhou's scenic West Lake. He first learned of the internet as an interpreter for a trade delegation to Seattle in 1995. Inspired, he returned home and set up a yellow pages-style listing of Chinese businesses. When his startup was absorbed through an ill-fated joint venture with a state-owned telecom business, he landed at a newly opened, government-supported e-commerce initiative for Chinese businesses. Two years into that post, acting on his entrepreneurial impulses, Ma gathered with 17 friends at his apartment, and pitched them on his idea of an online trade fair for China's mom-and-pop businesses. He convinced them to build Alibaba with him in 1999, when dozens of other internet startups were about to debut in China.

In 2014, Ma scored the largest-ever tech IPO on Wall Street. And the business he and his team built keeps climbing after setbacks that might have wrecked other companies.

Alibaba Gets Slapped

In 2020, at a peak in development, the planned IPO of Alibaba's fintech spinout, Ant Group, was suspended and its microlending business was curbed after founder Ma publicly criticized China's financial regulatory system as outdated and restrictive. The following year, Alibaba was fined $2.8 billion by Chinese authorities for antitrust violations—a show of

China's power over private enterprises and a signal to investors of the political risks in the communist country.

"The personality cult aspect of founders, the sort of Steve Jobs mold, became very dangerous in China," said Isaac Stone Fish, founder and CEO of New York–based Strategy Risks. "Chinese tech was always more successful the more government got out of the way, and tech is one of the only areas in the Chinese economy where private firms just dominate over state-owned firms."

Ma, who had stepped down as Alibaba chairman in 2019, gave up control of fintech giant Ant Group in 2023. He disappeared from public view for several months after the governmental crackdown, leading to speculation he had gone missing. It turned out he was spending his time abroad, teaching and working on philanthropic interests but keeping a close eye on Alibaba.

Meanwhile, Alibaba's core e-commerce business was getting clobbered by newcomer Pinduoduo, with its game-changing combination of social media and online shopping—or social commerce (see Chapter 8).

Dealing with tightening regulations over big tech and seeking to unlock innovation, the company was restructured into six decentralized businesses in 2023 that could each raise funds, scale up, and go public. A management shakeup saw two cofounders from Alibaba's 19-member original team take the helm. Alibaba cofounder Joe Tsai, the billionaire owner of the Brooklyn Nets and a longtime close associate of Ma, was prodded into returning in a hands-on role as chairman from his prior post as executive vice chairman. Eddie Wu, a key figure in developing several of the firm's core products, became CEO.

With the old guard in place, the company sought to return to its original startup culture. Ma exerted his influence, issuing an internal memo in late 2023 to rally the team and "correct course." Ma remains a major shareholder in Alibaba and has been repurchasing shares in the company along with chairman Tsai.

Digital and AI consultant Jeffrey Towson, a longtime Alibaba observer, has described the transitions as positive. "Things have really accelerated at Alibaba in the past year. New leadership. New organizational structure. New strategy. And it all looks really good," he noted. He pointed to several signs of progress: a refocus on the core e-commerce business, faster and cheaper delivery, integration of generative AI into shopping services, and big investment in Alibaba's cloud platform.[5]

Tencent Galloped Like a Horse

Tencent founder Ma Huateng (b. 1971)—"Pony Ma"—a press-shy engineer born and educated in southern China, has been described as a scorpion who will lie in wait before attacking. As chairman and CEO of Tencent, he has lived up to his go-getter reputation and the Tencent brand name, derived from a fusion of the Chinese characters *teng* and *xun*, which together mean "galloping fast information." It's best known for its Swiss Army-like WeChat messaging app in China and a winking penguin mascot. Tencent supersized to belong among the world's largest video gaming companies, up there with Sony, Microsoft, and Nintendo—a feat made possible in part by acquiring Los Angeles-based Riot Games in 2015 and Supercell in Finland in 2016.

Tencent's entertainment and communications colossus has been compared with Disney and WarnerMedia but more digital, more diversified in video, music, games, social networking, and content, and decidedly more Chinese. South African media and internet group Naspers owns 24 percent of Tencent shares, reduced from a 31 percent stake in 2018. The sell-down was interpreted as a way to avoid overexposure to Chinese tech—although Naspers has stated a long-term commitment to Tencent.

Tencent built its empire from southern China far from Los Angeles and New York, starting in 1998. Smart acquisitions, tech startup investments, and organic growth propelled it until the Chinese regulatory crackdown led Tencent to rethink a strategy of bigger is better.

Caught up in this sweep, Tencent divested from delivery service Meituan in a $20.3 billion deal in 2022. The year before, Tencent cut its stake in logistics leader JD.com, out as the largest shareholder. Tencent sold its 5 percent stake in Tesla in 2021, which it had acquired in 2017 for $1.78 billion.

Tencent was slapped too with relatively small fines for antitrust violations and data management issues. Its video gaming business also was hit with restrictions over additive and violent content, and number of viewing hours by children and teens. Chinese regulators froze approval of new online games in mid-2018. Tencent's gaming business has since rebounded with several successful game launches.

Surprise Comeback

Overall, the outlook for China's BAT is brightening, with improving financial results. This rebound has been labeled by Bloomberg as a "surprise comeback"—a change that followed the Chinese government introducing economic and financial boosters.[6] China's tech titans have learned how to respond "in China time" (meaning superfast) to market conditions, and are managing to stay ahead, and strategize for the future. No longer copying, they are sometimes even out-innovating the West.

The next chapter explores the second tier of tech titans that came after the BAT, and shows how they are shaping their own destiny. ByteDance, the maker of TikTok, is one of them.

CHAPTER 3

NEXT-GEN MOBILE APPS LEAPFROG OVER PC ERA

The next tier of Chinese tech leaders—TikTok owner ByteDance, Meituan, and Xiaomi—have leveraged China's vast mobile internet market to expand in China and are diversifying into entirely new fields and regions to spread their innovative skills more broadly.

During the boom years of China's tech industry, innovation moved so quickly that a new wave of upstarts soon followed the rise of Baidu, Alibaba, and Tencent. This next generation—ByteDance, Xiaomi, and Meituan—pushed boundaries with 15-second video sensations and AI-curated news, sleek smartphones and smart home devices rivaling Apple and Alexa, and super apps that outperformed services like Uber Eats and DoorDash.

Back in China's internet boom of the early 2000s, Chinese entrepreneur Wang Xing earned a reputation as the "cloner."

He launched a string of copycats of Facebook, Friendster, and Twitter tailored for Chinese users. None gained serious traction, but Wang didn't give up.

Instead, he kept iterating, learning from each misstep. His persistence finally paid off with the launch of Meituan, a group-buying platform inspired by Groupon, but which quickly evolved into something far more ambitious. Under Wang's leadership, Meituan expanded into food delivery, hotel bookings, travel services, and more, eventually becoming one of China's most essential everyday apps. What began as imitation grew into innovation, reflecting a broader shift in China's tech scene—from fast followers to global trailblazers. In the urban sprawl of Beijing, Shanghai, and Shenzhen, Meituan's fluorescent yellow-and-black-clad couriers—some 7.5 million nationwide—speed by on mopeds, commanding roughly 70 percent of China's food delivery.[1]

When the iPhone took off in China, Chinese tech entrepreneur Lei Jun was sometimes called the Steve Jobs of Apple. He launched China's smartphone Xiaomi in 2010 in the spirit of Jobs, mimicking not only Apple's designs but even Jobs's signature look—blue jeans, black T-shirt attire, and dramatic stage presence. At one launch event, Lei even echoed Jobs's famous line, teasing, "Just one more thing." When Xiaomi unveiled the Mi8 phone in 2018 to mark its eighth anniversary, critics called it the "most brazen iPhone copycat yet" for a near-identical look and features compared to the $1,000-priced iPhone X.

Today, Xiaomi has surpassed Apple to become China's top smartphone maker, and it consistently ranks second or third worldwide. No longer just a copycat, Xiaomi (pronounced *shao me*) has evolved into a powerhouse of consumer tech. It's built an ecosystem of connected electronics—from smart TVs and air purifiers to rice cookers and wearables—and is now making bold moves in electric vehicles. Its sleek SU7 sedan, priced at $30,620, was quickly followed by the sport utility vehicle YU7 in 2025 that soon sold out, aiming directly at Tesla's popular Model Y, and signaling Xiaomi's ambitions in mobile tech.

Chinese software engineer and serial entrepreneur Zhang Yiming, founder of ByteDance, recognized early on that digital media would eclipse newspapers. After a few early stumbles in entrepreneurship, he launched the AI-driven news aggregator Toutiao in 2012. The app delivers personalized content to 287 million daily readers, making it China's second-largest news platform after Tencent News[2]—though his international news app TopBuzz was shut down in 2020 after a five-year run.

Spotting the global shift toward video content as early as 2013, Zhang pivoted again—this time with transformative results. He launched video-sharing sites Douyin in China and its international twin, TikTok. What followed was explosive growth: TikTok surged to more than 1 billion users, including 170 million in the US,[3] while Douyin drew 752 million viewers in China. ByteDance, the parent company behind both platforms, quickly became a titan in the tech world, now ranked as the second most valuable privately held startup globally, just behind SpaceX.[4] With its addictive AI-curated content feeds, ByteDance didn't just ride the short-video wave—it helped create it.

These tech titans thrived thanks to a combination of timing, tenacity, and tactics. They rose during a pivotal moment when China's economy was embracing private enterprise, seizing the opportunity with relentless drive, sharp market instincts, and an appetite for bold moves. Capitalizing on China's mobile-first culture and the rapid adoption of digital payment systems, they built products tailored to fast-paced urban lifestyles, rolling out smart devices, user-centric apps, and new features with

Table 3.1

How China's next-tier titans stack up

Company	International reach	Strongest global markets	Notable feature
ByteDance	Very high	US, SEA, EU, LatAm.*	TikTok is a global juggernaut
Xiaomi	Very high	India, EU, LatAm., SEA	Huge smartphone exporter
Meituan	Low	China only	China-first, China-only

*EU = European Union; LatAm. = Latin America; SEA = Southeast Asia

Source: Silicon Dragon Ventures

remarkable speed. They carved out major shares in China's digital landscape—e-commerce, smartphones, video, food delivery. Xiaomi and ByteDance made a splash far beyond China with their innovations (see Table 3.1).

Bucking the Status Quo

These companies didn't just follow trends. They set them. By harnessing cutting-edge AI, powerful recommendation algorithms, seamless mobile payments, and real-time data analytics, they sometimes outpaced their Western counterparts. In fact, some of their product designs and digital strategies have been copied by American tech giants.

Together, these next-generation players represent the vanguard of a more confident and capable wave of homegrown Chinese innovation. These hyper-scalers have raised billions of venture capital—ironically, most of it from Western investors. Their rise has brought not only admiration but also scrutiny and controversy. While their roots and primary markets remain in China, their ambitions are largely international (Table 3.1).

Not all ventures have gone smoothly, especially outside China. Didi, the ride-hailing service once hailed as China's Uber killer, faced regulatory setbacks and was forced to delist from the New York Stock Exchange. Yet the company remains determined to rebound, signaling the perseverance that defines this new generation of Chinese tech leaders (see Chapter 7, A Not-so-Shared Economy).

It's unlikely that these Chinese tech giants will be unseated from their dominant positions within China's rapidly evolving tech sector. But it's equally unlikely they'll gain significant traction in the US market, TikTok being the rare exception.

Until the debate over a possible TikTok ban erupted, ByteDance remained relatively unknown in the West. Now, it's recognized as one of the most innovative tech firms not just in China but globally. ByteDance made its mark with a powerful algorithm that continually feeds users personalized news and video content—fueling the addictive nature of apps like Toutiao and TikTok.

Yet TikTok's Chinese origins have drawn intense scrutiny in the US, where concerns over national security and data privacy have put the app in political crosshairs. ByteDance, TikTok's parent company, has reportedly allowed Chinese Communist Party (CCP) officials to participate in its internal committees[5] —a common practice in China, where any company with over 50 employees typically includes a CCP presence, and those with over 100 must appoint party cell leaders who report to local authorities.[6]

The US government considered whether to ban or make a deal to sell its US arm to an American-led investor group. TikTok's explosive popularity was too large to simply erase. Meanwhile, the Chinese government was tightening influence over key tech players by acquiring so-called "golden shares"—small but powerful stakes that grant veto rights and boardroom access.

> *"President Trump may let the clock run out on a possible TikTok ban."*
>
> **Paul Triolo**
> Partner, DGA-Albright Stonebridge Group

Instead of forcing a sale or shutdown of TikTok, President Donald Trump was in effect "letting the clock run out". That was the assessment of tech policy expert Paul Triolo, a partner at consulting firm DGA-Albright Stonebridge Group. Under a law signed by former President Joe Biden, TikTok was given until January 19, 2025, to either sell to a US-approved buyer or face a nationwide ban. The law cited national security concerns tied to ByteDance's Chinese ownership. For a brief period, around that deadline for action, TikTok was effectively banned—service was halted—but it resumed just 14 hours later, following an executive order from Trump that allowed the app to continue operations. President Trump then postponed the deadline for a sale or block of TikTok. This delay added uncertainty to TikTok's future in the US, as the video platform operated in a gray zone—hugely popular among US users but caught in the geopolitical tug-of-war between Washington and Beijing.

In response to mounting concerns over US data privacy, TikTok has emphasized that it maintains distinct data systems and infrastructure for US operations, with American user traffic routed through Oracle servers, stored domestically, and monitored by a dedicated US-based team under an initiative known as Project Texas, launched in January 2023.[7]

Elsewhere, TikTok has faced similar backlash in other countries concerned about potential security risks and foreign influences. TikTok has been shut off in India since 2020. Several Western governments including the US, Canada, the UK, and European Union members have restricted TikTok on government-issued devices, citing national security risks and potential exposure of sensitive information.

Despite its reassurances and technical safeguards, TikTok remained at the center of a global debate over data sovereignty, digital trust, and the broader implications of Chinese tech influence on the world stage. Nevertheless, the app's meteoric (though controversial) rise in the West marks a historic leap for Chinese tech companies going global.

Google and Meta have scrambled to replicate TikTok's magic, launching short-form video features like YouTube Shorts and Instagram Reels. But TikTok remains a dominant force. Among Gen Z youngsters in the US, nearly two-thirds regularly use TikTok, placing it on par with Instagram and YouTube as a go-to destination, not just for entertainment but also news, shopping, and social connections.[8] What's more, TikTok has unexpectedly evolved into a major news source. Nearly half of US users routinely get headlines from the app,[9] highlighting its growing role as a gateway to current events and cultural trends. TikTok has redefined how a new generation consumes media, turning a Chinese-born platform into a cornerstone of digital life in the West.

Scaling on Dual Tracks

ByteDance founder Zhang made a strategically savvy decision early on: he created two distinct tracks—one for China and one for the rest of the world—as the company entered into livestreaming and short-form video. In 2016, ByteDance launched Douyin, specifically built for Chinese users. It operates on servers in China, features a Mandarin language interface, and, adhering to the country's internet governance, has built-in content filtering and real-name registration.

This dual-track approach allowed ByteDance to scale rapidly at home while avoiding the regulatory and reputational risks that might have come from mixing Chinese and international user data or content. It also gave the company the capacity to innovate independently for each market.

Douyin's international counterpart, TikTok, debuted a year later for a global audience. It featured a different content moderation system, broader cultural topics, and more lenient standards aligned with Western norms. Some of TikTok short-video features have even been copied by Silicon Valley's best (think Instagram Reels).

In China, Douyin has grown into a dominant player not just in video entertainment, but also in integrated e-commerce, livestreamed informercials, and payment services, earning a commission on each transaction.

Following a similar path, TikTok introduced social shopping to Western audiences. An acquisition of social video app Musical.ly, which had a large following in the US, helped TikTok to expand. TikTok has hosted as many as 7 million US businesses who use the app as a marketing tool and a place to sell products.[10]

Table 3.2

TikTok's rise globally and China

Year	Douyin (China)	TikTok (Global)
2020	600 million	800 million*
2025	766 million	1.59 billion
Growth (%)	+25.3	+91.3

*Monthly active users, early 2025

Source: Statista

ByteDance became one of China's first global internet success stories. Its separation of China and Western content and operations helped ByteDance navigate the complexities of cross-border tech. ByteDance was able to export a model that fused entertainment, commerce, and AI—a formula that the West is now imitating. It succeeded not just by translating a product but by re-engineering it for each market (see Tables 3.2 and 3.3).

That Awesome Algorithm

The popularity of ByteDance apps stems from the highly secretive and guarded AI recommendation algorithms that match videos with user interests, based on viewership patterns, likes and follows, and length of time over a piece of content.[11] TikTok's algorithm is widely considered to be the gold standard in grabbing user's attention and keeping them hooked. Videos of boyish pranks, dancing lessons, dog grooming tips, and lip-synching catch on among teens and millennials with little translation required.

Table 3.3

How China's Douyin compares with TikTok

Feature	Douyin	TikTok
Market	China only	Global (excluding main-land China)
Launched	2016	2017 (as international counterpart)
Platform owner	ByteDance	ByteDance
Servers/data	Hosted within China	Hosted internationally (Singapore, US)
Content rules	Follows China's censorship laws	Follows local laws in each country
Features	More advanced e-commerce and payments	Slowly integrating similar features

Source: Silicon Dragon Ventures

This algorithm was created by ByteDance founder Zhang (b. 1983), who grew up in the southern province of Fujian and graduated with a degree in computer engineering from Nankai University in Tianjin. After working briefly at Microsoft, he started travel booking site Kuxun, which was sold to TripAdvisor in 2009, then he ran real estate portal 99Fang.com and developed a train ticket app based on short-text messages. It wasn't until he dreamed up the idea of AI-powered content over mobile that he scored a big success with ByteDance.

I had little idea of its lofty value when meeting his first investor in Beijing, Joan Wang, managing director of SIG Asia, Susquehanna International Group's venture capital unit in China. An early supporter of Zhang in his prior ventures, she worked out a deal with him to invest a small amount in his AI news app startup in 2012, which resulted in the Philadelphia firm today owning a 15 percent stake in ByteDance, which would be worth nearly $50 billion based on recent valuations in an employee share buyback and more than $15 billion in 2020. After that initial deal at its founding, Sequoia Capital China and several private equity firms including General Atlantic, KKR, and Carlyle piled in. They've collectively invested $9.4 billion in ByteDance over multiple rounds. By riding the wave of China's mobile internet and AI boom as investors bet on the potential of ByteDance, young Chinese tech entrepreneur Zhang was named by *Forbes* as China's richest person with an estimated net worth of $65.5 billion.[12]

Given the geopolitical issues surrounding TikTok, investors with a stake in ByteDance, including several public pension funds, could have an illiquid investment that is difficult to sell. Moreover, ByteDance is unlikely to go public anytime soon, which would open its shares for investors to exit.

Like other Chinese tech giants, ByteDance got caught up in the Chinese government's crackdown in the early 2020s. In a move seen as a tightening grip over the country's internet sector, in 2021, the Chinese government took a 1 percent ownership of a ByteDance subsidiary that controls domestic Chinese news and information content online. Moreover, the AI app maker was hit with security investigations and fines related to data misuse, fake news, and offensive content such as celebrity gossip, vulgarity, and scandals. That sort of content, early in its growth, had earned founder Zhang the nickname, the King of Titillating Content.[13]

As his company grew, and the scrutiny and pressures of running a larger business heightened, Zhang stepped down as CEO in 2021.[14] That tough year for China's internet founders saw a wave of executive exits, including the resignation of Ant Group's

CEO Simon Hu after its IPO was halted and the departure of Pinduoduo founder Colin Huang to pursue personal interests in life sciences. Since leaving his post at ByteDance, the low-key Zhang has avoided the spotlight and redirected his focus to AI initiatives. In 2023, his profile rose again when he played a key role in launching Doubao, one of China's hottest AI chatbots.[15]

Xiaomi versus Apple

In several other markets where Chinese and American tech giants compete, China has proven a formidable challenger. Take Xiaomi, the smartphone maker. While smartphones represent more than half its revenues, Xiaomi has diversified and become a lifestyle tech and EV brand. It makes and sells internet-connected TVs, laptops, vacuum cleaners, rice cookers, fans, and smart watches, operates Mi retail stores online, and runs an e-commerce site. Of course, Apple has its own ecosystem of entertainment products, connected devices, and shops. But what it doesn't have is a car.

In 2024, Xiaomi launched its first electric vehicle (EV), the cool-looking Xiaomi SU7 sedan, then followed up a year later by adding a sport-utility vehicle to the lineup. The vehicles are so popular that fans line up and buy tickets to tour the company's highly automated EV factory in Beijing. These launches have put Xiaomi years ahead of Apple and its cancelled project to build an EV. Xiaomi has been able to succeed in EVs based upon engineering smarts, China's vast supply chain, and mastery of advanced manufacturing.

"Apple spent six years trying to bring a car to market. Apple fundamentally is a purely digital company. It makes a phone but the profit and products are driven by its operating systems. So its platform is a phone. Xiaomi had a phone, but it also had vacuum cleaners, and other robotics. Xiaomi learns how to deal with analog devices. A car is an analog device. All the things that make a car are things that Xiaomi has in its manufacturing ecosystem from day one. So that's how it could design a car," explained venture capitalist Gary Rieschel of Qiming Venture, an early Xiaomi investor in 2010.

A Bite out of Apple

The smartphone market remains a key battleground for China's innovators to attract and retain customers, and go global. Fueled by sleek designs and competitive pricing, Chinese smartphone makers now account for over half (56 percent) of global smartphone sales. "While their core markets remain China and Asia, these brands are rapidly expanding their footprint throughout Europe and Africa, driven by the strong performance of their low-end and mid-range devices," noted Francisco Jeronimo, vice president for EMEA Client Devices at IDC.[16]

In this increasingly crowded international market, Xiaomi has emerged as a major player, landing third place globally, trailing Samsung in the lead and Apple in second place.[17] Almost half of Xiaomi's revenues now comes from outside China, with India also a prime market, where the brand's affordability and feature-rich devices are key selling points.

In China's highly competitive environment, Xiaomi staged a comeback and recently overtook Apple to reclaim a sales lead for the first time in a decade.[18] Meanwhile, the iPhone has slipped, as a wave of lower-priced Chinese brands, buoyed by government subsidies, gained ground rapidly. Of the top five smartphones in China today—Xiaomi, Huawei, OPPO, and Vivo—only Apple is not Chinese, underscoring how dominant the domestic players have become in the world's largest smartphone market.

That Wild Card in Tech Trade

The Washington–Beijing trade conflict and knock-on trade and investment restrictions is a wild card for US and Chinese makers of everything from smartphones to automobiles. One pronounced example of the uncertainty played out recently in China's telecom market, when US export restrictions cut access to advanced chips and Google services to China in 2020.

Chinese tech conglomerate Huawei surprised the market by developing its own operating system, an Android alternative. It was a signal of China's drive for technological independence, showing that China could advance despite American roadblocks (though some experts questioned the extent of US technology used).[19]

Huawei's newish phone, the Mate 60 Pro, runs with a made-in-China chip and its homegrown HarmonyOS operating system. "Huawei is at the center of whole effort in China to do more domestically," observed tech expert and consultant Triolo. It's getting ready for more. Huawei has recently constructed a $1.4 billion R&D campus the size of a small city near Shanghai to do a deep dive into advanced chips, AI, and next-generation telecom standard 6G.

US Sales Off Limits

Xiaomi, too, is reducing its reliance on Silicon Valley, replacing Google's Android operating system with its homegrown MIUI, or "me, you, I," system. This local adaptation, HyperOS, integrates Xiaomi design and features.[20]

Xiaomi has epitomized the "made-in-China" stereotype of innovating fast and scaling up, with inexpensive but full-featured, high-quality products. Its foldable phones, super-thin models, extra-large screen displays, and all-ceramic phone casings have won over customers, dubbed "Mi fans," who provide feedback to new features in online forums and communities. Chinese consumers also love the prices, which are generally lower than iPhones in China, particularly for premium models.

The Xiaomi strategy of innovation, affordability, and localization has worked well in China and travels well globally. But there's one market where it hasn't been able to penetrate: the US. China's internet-connected EVs have been banned from the US due to national security concerns about data privacy.

Xiaomi phones can be bought on eBay or Amazon, but they don't come with official support and may not work because of US network bans. Also, the Chinese-made phones can be considered security risks. Yet, international business executives I know who go to China regularly boast about Xiaomi phones they have bought on recent trips and show them off in meetings with other globetrotters.

The Dual Advantage

Xiaomi founder Lei Jun (b. 1969) spent the early part of his career as an engineer at Chinese software maker Kingsoft in Beijing, rising to CEO in 1992, and later turning it into a mobile internet company. He channeled through several other promising startups as an investor and developer that became winners in China's burgeoning internet market. But Lei's biggest hit was in getting his entrepreneurial hands dirty with Xiaomi. His vision was to make and sell a well-designed, low-priced phone that would ride on China's emerging mobile internet market. He cofounded Xiaomi in 2010 with Lin Bin, a former Microsoft and Google engineer.

Xiaomi took off in 2010 from a small software company to a publicly traded giant with $52.6 billion in revenues. Lei's vision for his startup was clear: mobile phones would replace laptops and include daily customizable features based on social media feedback; sales channels would be direct-to-consumer. As he built Xiaomi, he stayed clued into the buzzing startup scene in Beijing, where I saw him blending in with Chinese and US entrepreneurs at tech events. His tech-infused business strategy for Xiaomi was compelling and creative. He described his "triathlon business model" consisting of three synergistic pillars of growth: handsets for the bulk of sales, Internet of Things (IoT) gadgets, and consumer goods as a complement, and lastly internet value-added services.

The Xiaomi advantage has been this combination of hardware and software anchors. Xiaomi may seem like a hardware company only with smartphone and smart TVs, but it's actually the "first internet-of-things company with an array of smart hardware devices," noted tech and media analyst Ben Thompson, founder of Stratechery.[21] He pointed out that Xiaomi was one of the rare companies to succeed in both hardware and software.

Xiaomi also effectively applies the razor-and-blade marketing scheme of selling one item at a low cost to increase sales of a complementary item. From the outset, Xiaomi kept the cost of its smartphones and smart household goods at a level that limited profit margins to only 5 percent. This helped to build up a customer base. Then it hooked those users on its multiple apps for music, videos, and games that are monetized with advertising, subscriptions, and virtual gifts. It was a lesson that Apple learned in integrating more revenue-producing, subscription-based entertainment and news content into iPhones—something Xiaomi did from day one.

The Delivery King Meituan

Another of China's standouts in this tier of titans is Meituan. It was created through a 2015 merger of Groupon-like group-buying site Meituan and Yelp-like Dianping.com. From AI and big data to robots and drones, this on-demand commerce and delivery service has kept leveraging China's digital age. It competes most directly with logistics giant JD.com, which began offering some similar food services. Founder Wang Xing, long ago leaving behind his cloner image, has turned his original food delivery business into a lifestyle super app—a made-in-China concept primed for the nation's mobile-first markets and popular with urban consumers for super-quick orders and deliveries of everyday essentials and treats. Meituan, which translates to "beautiful group" in Chinese, offers restaurant reviews, hotel bookings, and local reviews—Yelp, Booking.com, Grubhub, Uber Eats, and OpenTable all combined in one place.

Like other Chinese tech giants, Meituan has jumped into the AI race. In 2023, the company debuted a version of a ChatGPT-style chatbot and, two years later, launched a proprietary large language model (LLM) dubbed "LongCat." This AI tool, which builds upon its core business, provides food listings with flavor tags and portion descriptions, and relies on algorithms to personalize recommendations according to individual tastes and past shopping.

Delivery is getting smarter, too. In several cities, Meituan drones lift off from rooftops, flying packages to pick-up kiosks below. On the ground, self-driving delivery robots equipped with heated and cooled compartments navigate sidewalks, handing off meals within meters of buyers' doors. These robots operate like a mobile vending machine where customers can order, pay, and unlock their meals with a code.

Behind the scenes, Meituan's engine runs on big data. Advanced technology charts optimal delivery routes in real time to dodge traffic jams and avoid accident sites, and helps dispatchers make quick decisions. An intelligent voice assistant lets couriers report updates or receive new assignments without glancing at a screen.

Other techie stuff Meituan has built into the platform is for security and compliance. Couriers verify themselves with QR codes. A backend data system checks merchant licenses against official government records and tracks food safety. Customer reviews are analyzed by timeframe, location, and product category to catch any potential issues.

A Quick Stop at HQ

At the bustling northeast Beijing corporate headquarters of Meituan, you can't miss a large billboard promoting the company's feel-good mission statement: "Help people eat better, live better." A large showroom in the extensive lobby displays screens documenting the company's evolution from group-buying startup in 2010 to merge with rival restaurant review and dining site Dianping to richly funded unicorn with big-name backers to publicly traded company. The huge digital screens give a good overview of the company's leadership of the delivery service market, which sprang up in China with urbanization, technology development, widespread mobile internet usage, and increased consumer spending. On a visit there back in 2018, I saw how Meituan stacks up in China and compares with Uber in the US for features (see Table 3.4). In 2018, Meituan packed in more than 200 service and product categories and racked up 357 million active buyers annually, 5.1 million merchants in 2800 Chinese cities, 5.8 billion transactions, and 5 billion user reviews.[22] The upside seemed clear.

Meituan went public in Hong Kong in 2018 and, riding on the digital economy, saw revenues nearly double to $46.1 billion since 2020. Underlying that growth, however, were signs of weakness—net losses in 2021 and 2022. It's been tough dealing with COVID restrictions, fierce competition and a price war with rivals, JD and Alibaba-acquired service Ele.me, which, like Meituan, was similar to Uber Eats (see Table 3.4). Regulatory pressures also proved a challenge such as the Chinese government's $530 million fine for monopolistic practices,

Table 3.4

How Chinese and US delivery apps compare

Feature	Meituan	Uber Eats
Ecosystem	Full super app	Delivery-focused
Service range	Very broad	Narrower
Tech & logistics	Advanced (robots)	Solid AI
Innovation speed	High	Moderate
Global presence	Focused in China	Global

Source: Silicon Dragon Ventures

which included a requirement for merchants to work with one provider. Plus, the company was struggling financially, investing heavily in autonomous delivery and AI while its core food delivery business remained labor intensive and cash-burn-heavy. Other drags resulted from its community group-buying business of low-cost bulk orders popular outside city centers. Meanwhile, in 2022, Meituan lost a major backer, when Tencent shed most of its 17 percent stake in Meituan valued at $24 billion, a move seen partly as a response to China's regulatory crackdown on too-big tech companies.

Unlike other Chinese tech giants that expanded internationally, Meituan does not have that cushion. Only in China, where consumer spending has slowed, its market valuation has been dropping from an all-time high in early 2021. But don't count Meituan out.

The Internet Cloner

From Fujian province in southeastern China, a part of the country known for its successful small business culture, Meituan founder Wang Xing (b. 1979) has become one of China's richest individuals, with a net worth of $10.2 billion,[23] primarily derived from his 9.2 percent stake in his startup. Wang earned a bachelor's degree in electronic engineering degree from China's MIT, Tsinghua University, then went to the US for a master's degree in computer science at the University of Delaware in 2005, but dropped out of PhD studies there to return home. Inspired by the success of Facebook, he embarked on a winding entrepreneurial path during the rise of the internet in China. He faced many setbacks; Meituan has been his victory so far. As Wang says in a poetic way about his journey, "The more faithful we are to the future, the more patient we are."

For clues to how he got that cloner image, consider the following. His first effort at building a social network, a basic copy of early social networking site Friendster named Duoduoyou, didn't catch on. Then his Facebook copy Xiaonei was popular with users but burned through cash quickly and was sold to Oak Pacific Interactive for $2 million in 2006 and renamed Renren. His next try was Fanfou, a popular Twitter copy. But Fanfou was taken offline for 18 months by Chinese government censors in 2009 during a series of violent riots in western China. Meanwhile, Fanfou was soon overtaken when NASDAQ-listed Chinese high-flier Sina Corp. launched microblogging website Sina Weibo.

The entrepreneurial programmer Wang was taking a cue from Silicon Valley that it's OK to fail many times when he ventured on to launch Meituan in 2010. Meituan actually began as a copy, too, of US group discount-buying site Groupon. That wasn't a sure bet, either.

At the time, Groupon lookalikes were springing up throughout urban China in what was labeled the Battle of a Thousand Groupons, all chasing China's bargain-loving consumers. Big-time investors Alibaba and Tencent and several Chinese venture heavyweights poured millions into the copycats eager to cash in on the craze. The original Groupon also joined the fray in 2011 in a joint venture, Gaopeng, with Tencent in China. From 2010 to 2014, Meituan bulked up with large venture capital rounds from international investors while its lead rival, Dianping, did the same and also gained Tencent as a major backer.

In this battles, lines were drawn over larger and larger advertising budgets, bigger and bigger subsidies, and higher-value coupons offering 60 percent discounts. The lead contenders, Meituan and Dianping, kept raising more capital but costly marketing expenses took a toll. The original Groupon China actually flopped, a déjà vu of earlier attempts by eBay, Yahoo, and Google in China to win against fierce local rivals. Meanwhile, survivors Meituan and Dianping continued to fight it out with more capital: Meituan pulled in $700 million in 2015 and Dianping $850 million the same year.

A Golden Week Merger

It was China's Golden Week when a truce was finally called. Meituan merged with its top rival, Dianping, in a $15 billion transaction supported by their big-name backers Alibaba, Tencent, and Sequoia Capital China. The merger was a good fit—a mashup of Meituan's Groupon-type vouchers for movie tickets and travel bookings and its food delivery service with the restaurant reviews and listings of Yelp-like Dianping. Wang took charge of the merged leader. Soon, he roped in several of his prior cofounders from the internet era, and raised $4 billion from Tencent and the Priceline Group (renamed Booking Holdings) in the US. That financing valued the Chinese services app at $30 billion, making it the world's third most valuable unicorn. In the end, Meituan emerged as China's leader in the "Internet Plus" market, or a combination of online and offline worlds known in China as O2O, the hottest buzzword of its time.

Founder Wang could easily retire and lie on a beach somewhere, but he still keeps chugging away at molding Meituan. He's brought Meituan across the border to Hong Kong and to the Middle East, to Riyadh. In Hong Kong, his food delivery drones go around mountains and across water, making for speedy trips.

His bigger priority is, you guessed it, AI! Meituan, like other tech titans, has developed its own LLM, "Longcat," competing with ByteDance's Doubao and Alibaba's Qwen (see Chapter 6).

This is a long way from the internet boom. By building their own LLMs, Chinese tech giants aim to decrease their dependence on Open AI or DeepMind, and fine-tune them for specific market sectors with language and cultural nuances. This trend, as it gains momentum, points to a further technological split between China and the West in a superpower competition for the future.

Currents have taken these tech titans into rocky terrain yet they are still determined to succeed within their own broader region and the so-called Global South. The next chapter looks at how regulations and geopolitical headwinds have blocked China dealmakers from getting into the US, and the US from getting into China.

CHAPTER 4

A REVOLVING DOOR SHUTS ON US–CHINA TECH DEALS

Dealmaking between the US and China is slowing down as geopolitical tensions intervene to nearly halt cross-border mergers, acquisitions, and joint ventures, and curb investment in startups. This is just one aspect of decoupling.

A New York–based partner at a major multinational auditing firm was on a business trip to Beijing, his first in a while. It was a tiring day of meetings with his client and colleagues, and he was looking forward to having a drink at the hotel bar he had frequented so much in the past. Though it was springlike weather and the streets were packed, the lobby of the hotel near the Forbidden City was eerily empty and the bar was closed.

While this was a letdown, he shouldn't have been surprised. The troublesome business environment over geopolitical issues and the near-three-year lockdown led many expatriates to return home to the US. When they do go back for meetings, their firms require them to travel with a "burner" prepaid cell phone with no personal or corporate identity and laptops that have been wiped clean.

Several restaurants and coffee shops in China's busy cities where US dealmakers used to hang out or discuss deals have closed for business—because business isn't what it used to be. Lawyers, accountants, and dealmakers are far less busy today than the prior boom-time decades. In Silicon Valley, the slowdown in cross-border US–China investment has freed up time but has been depressing. Venture capitalists and dealmakers who once merrily were active in China began to ponder their future over golf outings, skiing vacations, and meals in Palo Alto. Others retired early, their fortunes already made when R&D collaboration and money were flowing freely across the Pacific.

Even entrepreneurial founders in the Valley were now rejecting capital that had any hint of Chinese. Shenzhen-founded generative AI startup HeyGen pivoted from China and relocated to Los Angeles. Co-founder Joshua Xu reportedly asked his Chinese venture investors,[1] including Baidu Ventures, IDG Capital, ZhenFund, and former Sequoia China firm HongShan to offload shares of his AI video startup to US firms so he could avoid China connections and attract more stateside capital. American tech investor Sarah Guo took over HongShan's board seat in a $5.6 million investment deal led by her firm Conviction Capital. This is just one example of shuffle in US–Chinese transactions.

In this breakup of US and China dealmaking, at least 13 US law firms have closed or downsized their offices in Shanghai, Beijing, or Hong Kong,[2] including prominent ones such as Skadden, Morrison & Foerster, Paul Weiss, and Sidley Austin. Several partners of American law firms who were supporters of my work Silicon Dragon Ventures, have relocated and now live in Los Angeles or San Francisco—and look more Hollywood or Silicon Valley all the time. They rarely travel to China. In the hyped-up period of the 2010s, nearly all firms in Silicon Valley had at least one startup active in China as a client. Now, the action has wound down, and it's about getting out.

This is quite the contrast to a decade ago, when US–China deals kept everyone scurrying. China challenged the world with innovations and hard work and then became a threat to US tech dominance. Washington pushed back on China's advances with export controls and investment restrictions. Sand Hill Road–style deals with Chinese tech startups nearly came to a halt, particularly in so-called sensitive sectors that have both consumer and military uses such as GPS trackers, AI sensors, and facial recognition.

Investment deal-tracking reveals the depth of the cross-border decline in this geopolitically charged environment surrounding many high-tech sectors:

- Cross-border China–US venture investment fell to 14 percent out of a total 14,320 deals in 2024, from 27 percent in 2020.[3]
- US private equity and venture capital investment in China dropped to $4 billion across 48 deals, the lowest point in a decade.[4]
- Chinese investment in the US plunged from a peak of $46 billion in 2016 to less than $5 billion in 2022.[5] State-backed groups such as the China Investment Corporation cut off new investment in US private equity and no longer makes commitments to American funds.[6] Chinese funds also are seeking to be excluded from investments in individual US portfolio companies.

- Chinese merger and acquisition deals in the US dropped to their lowest level in 10 years while China's corporate dealmakers instead favored Asia as well as Brazil and Africa.[7]
- Domestic M&A deals grew within the world's second-largest economy, as state-owned enterprises consolidated to improve their competitiveness in industrial sectors of national interest such as the recent mega-merger within China's shipbuilding industry.[8]
- In a drought of public market listings, only 98 company IPOs in Mainland China raised $8.9 billion in 2024, the lowest number in a decade—as tightened regulations kicked in and fewer potential listings were approved.[9]

Dealing with a New Foe

In the past, the US successfully contested a modern technological competitor, Japan. Now China's growing strength represents a greater challenge. Over the past decade, worries about China over national security, data privacy, unfair advantages—and most of all—tech progress have fractured US–China relations. Where research and development collaboration, cross-border investment, interconnected supply chains, and technology interdependence existed, a techno-nationalist wall has risen. A so-called splinternet or technological decoupling has developed between these tech superpower nations of the world—the US and China.

"The fact is that America has been technologically dominant for so long that some US leaders came to take it for granted. They were wrong. A second technological superpower, China, has emerged," former Google CEO Eric Schmidt has pointed out.[10] He predicted as early as 2018 that the global internet would "bifurcate into a Chinese-led internet and a US-led internet." Back then, "this idea was still novel enough that the comment made headlines around the world," he noted in a report on US–China decoupling by the Carnegie Endowment for International Peace. "Now, the prediction has already come halfway true."

"We cannot afford to muddle through technological decoupling, one of the most consequential global trends of the twenty-first century," wrote Jon Bateman, a senior fellow and co-director of the Technology and International Affairs Program at the Carnegie center. He asked how far the US government should go with technology restrictions before they do more harm than good to America?[11]

It's a good question. There's strong evidence that US restrictions are causing China to try harder to become self-reliant from semiconductors to AI to robotics. The Chinese government has begun requiring companies to replace American AI software and semiconductor chips with homegrown versions.[12]

The Dragon Breathes Fire

Low costs, growing innovation prowess, and a government intent on technology dominance have made China a formidable challenger to the US, or as one Washington-based think tank on global policy has declared, "a fire-breathing dragon on government-provided steroids." Obviously, the rhetoric has run strong. Robert D. Atkinson, founder and president of the Information Technology & Innovation Foundation in Washington, DC, concludes:

> The last decade has shown that China can be a globally competitive producer of technologically complex goods, such as telecom equipment, machine tools, computers, solar panels, high-speed rail, ships, drones, satellites, heavy equipment, and pharmaceuticals. In all these industries, China has gained significant global market share—and it is making rapid strides in emerging industries such as robotics, AI, quantum computing, and biotech.[13]

While the $250 billion US CHIPs and Science Act in 2022 was designed to help restore America's industrial decline and boost its semiconductor sector, Atkinson and others have argued that the US has been fighting back with defensive measures largely centered on national security concerns rather than preserving "US techno-economic capabilities."

These "derisking" policies of the US may not be all that effective in restraining China. Separate spheres of tech power are resulting, and the Chinese are proving quite capable in developing their own technologies and gaining an edge in some key sectors. The HarmonyOS system for newer smartphone models was specifically developed to skirt US export restrictions on chips and reduce reliance on American-made iOS and Android systems for direct access to essential components. China's HarmonyOS is becoming a third operating system alongside the American ones. In social media, Chinese and American brands have long existed in separate worlds due to censorship and data privacy issues (see Table 4.1). Now this decoupling is spanning across several other important sectors such as semiconductors and AI.

Table 4.1

How social media brands stack up in separate spheres

US brand	2020	2025	Growth (%)	Chinese brand	2020	2025	Growth (%)
Facebook	2,700	3,049	+12.9%	WeChat	1,165	1,336	+14.7%
YouTube	2,000	2,491	+24.6%	Douyin	600	752	+25.3%
WhatsApp	2,000	2,000	0%	Tencent QQ	617	574	-7.0%
Instagram	1,000	2,000	+100%	Kuaishou	400	685	+71.3%
TikTok	800	1,526	+90.8%	Weibo	511	582	+13.9%
Snapchat	500	750	+50%	Xiaohongshu	300	300	0%
Twitter	330	619	+87.6%	**Total users***	934	1,100	+17.8%
Total users	223	253	+13.5%				

*User figures in millions

Notes: MAU = monthly average users; Total users = overall number of social media users in the US, not the sum of individual platforms

Source: Industry reports, Statista, media coverage, annual reports

Ranking China Strategy Risks

Larger US companies are reevaluating the risk and financial returns of doing business in China, mindful of the heightened geopolitical conflicts, and inherent supply chain challenges of being too dependent on Chinese production. New York–based advisory Strategy Risks has recently ranked US companies by their exposure or ties to China. GM and Ford were high on that list, owing to their joint ventures with state-owned entities for auto manufacturing, according to the firm's founder Isaac Stone Fish. Carrier, Apple, and Tesla also were in the top tier on that scorecard for their vast operations in China. He's seeing a trend among US companies to appoint a chief risk officer and boards to monitor China involvement. "We have to remember that in China, politics dominates, and Beijing's goals aren't to create a flourishing market economy, but to ensure state control and a state-dominated economy, and to ensure that the party stays in power."

The fissures over national security concerns run deep. In early 2023, Ford Motor was planning to build a new $3.5 billion plant in Michigan with China's lithium-ion battery maker CATL. The deal was structured, not as a joint venture, but as a licensing deal with the world-leading Chinese battery company providing technology and equipment and with Ford owning the plant. Ford has since scaled back production plans amid uncertainty about EV demand in the US and higher costs, but the auto maker still plans to go ahead with a downsized plant with CATL and begin operation in 2026.

At this time of rising tensions, Chinese–US joint ventures on American soil are starting to be viewed as a pragmatic solution for economic cooperation. Mitch Presnick, a former visiting fellow at Harvard's Fairbank Center for Chinese studies and the founder of Super8 Hotels China, has contended that reshoring US manufacturing through joint ventures with Chinese multinationals would restore US technological competitiveness by tech transfer of China's battery-making skills, for instance, and would help to rebuild US supply chains in advanced, strategic industries such as electric vehicles, solar panels, and robotics.[14]

Presnick cited the example of a 2023 deal made between Chinese solar equipment maker Longji and US renewable developer Invenergy to invest $600 million to build a factory in Ohio through a China–US joint venture. This plant, Illuminate USA, has employed 1,000 workers.

Where have the IPOs gone?

Despite some signs of collaboration, China–US tensions continue to flare up in business and tech policy circles. On Wall Street, Chinese companies trading on New York exchanges periodically crops up as an issue that could lead to their removal. Talk has swirled of possible delistings of Chinese stocks. What a change from 2014 when Alibaba's IPO raised $25 billion on the NYSE, the largest ever!

Increased scrutiny by Washington has led to speculation that US-listed Chinese companies could be forced to delist.[15] If a full-scale decoupling of Chinese and US financial interests occurred, Goldman Sachs has warned that US investors would have to unload as much as $800 billion in Chinese equities.[16]

As many as 286 Chinese companies are trading on New York City exchanges with a total market capitalization of $1.1 trillion—including 48 Chinese IPO newcomers in 2024, according to a tally by the US–China Economic and Security Review Commission.[17] All Chinese state-owned enterprises (SOEs) have already delisted from American exchanges—the last two were China Eastern Airlines Corporation and China Southern Airlines Company in February 2023, following six Chinese SOEs that voluntarily left the year before. A chief reason for their exit: a regulatory agreement in 2022 between Beijing and Washington that granted the Public Company Accounting Oversight Board access to inspect the audit work of Chinese companies listed on US exchanges.

Jonathan Krane, founder and CEO of KraneShares, a New York-based asset management company that runs an exchange-traded fund tracking China stocks, told clients in April 2025 that a full-scale delisting is "low probability." But in the unlikely event, he informed them that his firm would convert its remaining US holdings to Hong Kong-traded shares of US-listed Chinese companies. In an earlier round of delisting concerns in 2022, KraneShares started shifting the bulk of those holdings to Hong Kong.[18]

Yet, despite the frictions, the past year has seen several higher-profile and successful Chinese IPOs on New York exchanges: EV maker Zeekr in a $441 million IPO, and autonomous driving startups WeRide at $440.5 million, and Pony. AI at $260 million—even Chinese bubble tea company Chagee! went public on Nasdaq.

Most of these newcomers, however, are small-cap issuers, rather than the previous multi-billion blockbuster IPOs of the early 2020s (such as ride-hailing company DiDi Global's $4.4 billion debut in New York and withdrawal (see Chapter 7).

The average Chinese IPO in 2024 raised just $50 million in proceeds, a sharp decline from $300 million in 2021. This decline reflects heightened geopolitical tensions and Beijing's greater control and oversight of overseas fundraising activities. Smaller Chinese listings in the US have been under recent scrutiny by the Securities and Exchange Commission for so-called pump and dump schemes while at the same time Beijing has put the brakes on Chinese companies seeking to go public in New York.[19]

"I don't think we're going to see an opening the floodgates for Chinese tech IPOs in the States. I think they're going to look to other markets, especially Hong Kong. I feel like the era of big tech Chinese IPOs in the States is over," observed geopolitical risks expert Fish.

Cholly-wood, anyone?

It wasn't long ago—2014–19—that a pipeline of China to US deals was very full. China's internet dragons invested heavily in tech startups in Silicon Valleys of the US. This was the promised land of innovation, and Chinese acquirers were eager to claim their part of it (see Tables 4.2 and 4.3).

Table 4.2

A sampling of Tencent's investments in US tech companies

2013			
Activision Blizzard	$2.3 billion	5% stake	interactive entertainment
Epic Games	$330 million	48% stake	video game and software
Fab.com	$150 million	coinv.*	online home décor
2015			
Riot Games	$400 million	acq.*	game developer
Glu Mobile	$126 million	inv.* 15%	game developer
Pocket Gems	$150 million	inv. (+2017)	mobile video game
2017			
Smule	$54 million	lead inv.	karaoke app
Snap	$2 billion	12% stake	video messaging app
Uber	$1.25 billion	coinv.	ride-hailing
Tesla	NA	5% stake	electric vehicle maker
Grail	$900 million	joint inv.	cancer detection
Essential Products	$300 million	inv.	consumer electronics
VoxelCloud	$15 million	lead inv.	medical AI
Locus Bioscience	$5 million	coinv.	biotech
2018			
Hammer & Chissel	$150 million	coinv.	game developer
Capture Technologies	$1 million	coinv.	event data analytics
Marble	$10 million	coinv.	robotic delivery
Skydance Media	und.*	inv.	film/VR
2019			
Reddit	$300 million	coinv.	social news aggregator

*acq. = acquisition; coinv. = coinvestor; inv. = investor; und. = undisclosed

Source: *Tech Titans of China*, 2019, Table 2.5; Silicon Dragon, S&P Global Market Intelligence, company reports

Table 4.3

A sampling of Alibaba investments in US tech startups

Smartrac	**inv.***	**und.***	**RFID, IoT**	**2018**
OpenSky	acq.*	und.	B2B e-commerce	2018
NVXL Technology	inv.	$20 million	machine learning	2017
EyeVerify	acq.	$100 million	security	2016
Snap	inv.	$200 million	photo app	2015
Lyft	coinv.*	$250 million	ridesharing	2014
Quixey	coinv.	$110 million	mobile search	2013–15
Tango.me	coinv.	$280 million	messaging app	2014
Kabam	inv.	$120 million	gaming	2014

* acq. = acquisition; coinv. = coinvestor; inv. = investor; und. = undisclosed

Source: *Tech Titans of China,* 2019, Table 2.4; Silicon Dragon, S&P Global Market Intelligence, company reports

Even Park Avenue and Hollywood were not too far. Anbang paid $1.95 billion in 2014 to buy Hilton's landmark Waldorf Astoria hotel on New York City's Park Avenue. The Chinese acquirer subsequently collapsed under heavy debt and was taken over by authorities through formation of a new entity, Dajia Insurance Group. Notably, the landmark hotel, under Chinese ownership, has been undergoing renovations for nearly nine years and finally reopened in 2025.

China's embrace of Tinseltown culture represented the country's bid for soft power in America's most iconic field and eagerness to create its own Hollywood-like studios and productions—*Chollywood*? China's Dalian Wanda Group acquired US movie theatre operator AMC and purchased film production company Legendary Pictures in Burbank. The Chinese conglomerate also built the largest movie studio in the world in the northern port city of Qingdao and lured foreign producers to shoot films, including *The Great Wall* starring Matt Damon in 2015. But since then, Wanda has cut its overseas holdings and turned focus to supporting the domestic Chinese film market. The debt-ridden Chinese group sold Legendary Entertainment Pictures, purchased for $3.5 billion in 2016, and offloaded movie studio operator AMC Entertainment, acquired in 2012 in a deal valued then at $2.6 billion.

Deal Alerts

China's internet dragons Baidu, Alibaba, and Tencent, which were such dominant dealmakers in the US, also scaled back their overseas ambitions and refocused on their home country.[20] The backdrop again was geopolitical tensions.

More pressure could be coming. President Trump's America First Investment Policy has outlined broader review of foreign (Chinese) in tech. In an alert to clients, law firm Wilson Sonsini spelled out that investors and companies should expect a likely expansion of rules governing cross-border investments and transactions, and advised clients to closely monitor new rulemaking by the US Department of the Treasury, specifically the Committee on Foreign Investment in the United States (CFIUS).

CFIUS has raised its head before, when reviewing transactions where a foreign entity acquires control or minority stakes in US critical technology, infrastructure, and sensitive personal data such as health and financial info. Several deals have been blocked over national security concerns. One was a joint venture between US robotics company Ekso Bionics and

Chinese company Zhejiang Youchang. They planned to build a facility in Zhejiang and manufacture exoskeleton personal mobility products integrating Ekso's technology so they could be sold in Chinese and other Asian markets. But the US company's prior work for the US government and concerns about technology transfers raised an alert. CFIUS objections led the joint venture to be terminated in 2020. Now Ekso Bionics is developing products in a former Ford factory building at its headquarters Richmond, California.

In another instance, in 2019, CFIUS required Chinese gaming company Kunlun to divest its investment stake in LGBTQ dating app Grindr. The issue here was national security concerns that Kunlun's engineers had access to US personal user data such as private messages. Grindr was sold in 2020 to an American company San Vicente Acquisition and in 2022, it went public via a SPAC (special purpose acquisition company) on the NYSE, establishing full American decision-making.

This transaction was seen as a possible precedent for TikTok parent company, ByteDance, and US regulators that were dealing with a possible ban or divestiture of its popular video-sharing site from Chinese ownership.[21] There is never a dull moment when it comes to China dealmaking.

Read on to the next section about the wild ride that US and China venture capital has been on in the past few years.

part two

SILICON DRAGON-STYLE VENTURE CAPITAL GETS SWEPT UP IN CROSSCURRENTS

CHAPTER 5

A NOT-SO-GOLDEN ERA FOR CROSS-PACIFIC VENTURE CAPITAL

Currents run strong across the Pacific to stop the flow of venture investments as Beijing and Washington exert more control. Once active, cross-border venture capital (VC) firms such as Sequoia Capital and GGV Capital have been forced to make a choice between China and the US. Many top venture capitalists have turned away from former hunting grounds in Chinese startup hubs and instead are scouting in Stanford and Berkeley or separately in Tsinghua and Fudan for the next new thing. This chapter also serves as a look at who's who among the leading venture investors in China, and how they have restructured in this new era.

Kai-Fu Lee had the room spellbound. The legendary tech investor—who once ran Google in China before forming his own venture firm—had flown in from Beijing and was giving a keynote speech. It was the annual HYSTA conference in Silicon

Valley, a gathering of Chinese American entrepreneurs hungry for insights. Lee, visiting from Beijing, confidently spoke about his latest work in AI and his VC firm, Sinovation Ventures. When I asked a question from the audience about the condition of China's entrepreneurial market, Lee's tone shifted. He acknowledged that it was "hibernating," though he quickly added, "It will come back more strongly than ever."

Not everyone shares Lee's optimism. The once-thriving ecosystem of Chinese startups and venture investors—which gave rise to Baidu, Alibaba, and Tencent—no longer seemed a boundless frontier. Investment dollars dried up. Beijing's tighter grip on big tech chilled innovation. Evolving geopolitics between the US and China caused Sand Hill Road's elite to pause or stop their bets in Chinese tech startups.

After Lee's speech, a young entrepreneur from China approached me, eager for introductions to US investors to fund his startup. But I had to tell him a hard truth. Few, if any, major venture firms were willing to take the risk on a Chinese startup—if they even could under new US restrictions. It was a stark change from the boom time when Silicon Valley's capital fueled China's brightest ideas.

Venture investor Feng Deng, whose Silicon Valley startup NetScreen had been acquired for $4 billion in 2004, understood the shift better than most. Running Northern Light Venture Capital in Beijing since 2005, he had coined a phrase that defined the new reality: "In China for China." The days when founders, ideas, capital, markets, and exits flowed between Beijing and Silicon Valley were gone. Today, the approach is nationalistic. While he and others have predicted that these hubs will collaborate again, many are not so sure.

The world's two largest VC markets have been undergoing a seismic transformation. In China, the government is pouring renminbi into industrial innovation, determined to create national champions. Meanwhile, in the US, Sand Hill Road investors are busily funding the next new thing (often AI) and regard China tech startups as a potential threat to their innovation lead.

Back in the "Silicon Dragon" days of 2000–19 (as I dubbed them), Silicon Valley's elite—Sequoia, GGV Capital, Lightspeed, Mayfield, NEA—poured millions into Chinese startups and fueled a golden era that gave rise to China's tech titans. The momentum seemed unstoppable. These Silicon Dragon investors inked well-timed deals with Chinese tech innovators in electric vehicles, video sharing apps, biotech, ride-hailing, smartphones, and fast-fashion e-commerce. Those days are over. One by one, Silicon Valley firms have separated out their China dealmaking and divested from Chinese portfolio companies, if they could find buyers.

On the *Forbes* Midas List of top 100 venture capitalists globally in tech, investors from Beijing, Shanghai, and Hong Kong placed high year after year. While perhaps not turning everything they touch into gold like the mythological King Midas, 14 China-based venture capitalists made the most recent rankings and even more in prior years (22 in 2020 and 18 in 2024).[1] Hong Kong–based Neil Shen, who is practically synonymous with Chinese startup investing, has aced this list several times and came in first four times. Previously known as a "steward" at Sequoia Capital, Shen, now head of separated investment firm HongShan, has backed many standout Chinese startups, among them TikTok owner ByteDance, delivery king Meituan, fast-fashion e-retailer Shein, and online marketplace Temu—all highlighted elsewhere in this book.

DC Cracks Down on Silicon Dragon Firms

The days of US-based venture firms profiting from well-placed bets on China tech startups are gone. In January 2025, new rules came into effect that put civil and criminal penalties on US entities that invest in Chinese companies in AI systems, semiconductors, and quantum computing that could be used by the military.

The Washington pushback on venture capital was triggered by research from Georgetown University's Center for Security and Emerging Technology, which scoped out US VC investment in Chinese tech.[2] What followed was a congressional investigation in 2023 that zeroed in on five major Silicon Valley firms that had invested billions into China's cutting-edge tech. The Select Committee on the Chinese Communist Party (CCP), chaired by then-Representative Mike Gallagher (now a defense contract executive at Palantir Technologies), published a telling report in February 2024.[3] The following were among its findings:

- More than $3 billion was invested into Chinese companies that "supported the PRC's [People's Republic of China] military, enabled human rights abuses, and allowed this rival nation to develop its own semiconductor market—an industry that the CCP sees as vital to its authoritarian goals."
- More than $1.9 billion was injected in AI companies in the PRC.
- $1 billion went to more than 150 PRC semiconductor firms.
- All five firms have US-based investors—limited partners that include university endowments, family offices, and pension funds.
- The five VCs provided expertise, global networks, reputational benefits, and access to global talent for their Chinese portfolio companies.

The conclusion: "If we continue on our present course, instead of seeing innovation championed by American companies, we will instead witness the CCP and their state-sponsored firms gaining control of critical technologies that will drive the next century of economic growth."

The committee issued several recommendations aimed at tightening restrictions on investments in Chinese entities linked to the military and forced labor programs, and formalizing limits on US investment in China's critical and emerging technologies.

Amid these growing pressures, some of the US VC firms expressed hesitation about cooperating with the investigation, noting direct or indirect pressure from the CCP. In some cases, their portfolio companies and limited partners urged them not to cooperate, fueling their reluctance to participate—although all five did. The VCs explicitly stated that their investments were made "during an era of optimism that lasted 15 years" and "coincided with expressed government policies and public positions in the US that encouraged businesses to invest in the region."[4]

Managing partners of the five VC investors under investigation by the Select Committee—GGV Capital, GSR Ventures, Walden International, Qualcomm Ventures, and Sequoia Capital—received letters with detailed inquiries about their China investments. Sources of capital, due diligence procedures, influence and control measures, and risk assessment factors were questioned, and requests were made about specific deals.[5]

GGV Capital was asked about funding for AI-powered facial recognition startup Megvii Technology. Qualcomm Ventures was probed for backing SenseTime, which was blacklisted in 2019 by the US for human rights abuses. At time of writing, GGV has been seeking to divest from Megvii and has divested from ByteDance and Xiaomi, according to the firm. Qualcomm divested from SenseTime in 2022.

GSR Ventures was also targeted for investing in at least 33 China AI startups, including Horizon Robotics and iFlyTek, and for backing Chinese semiconductor companies, which the Select Committee noted is a top priority of the CCP.

Walden's deals were pinpointed, too. The committee noted that at least 30 percent of the firm's AI investments were in PRC companies. Singled out was Walden's investment of more than $50 million in China's largest semiconductor foundry, SMIC, which had been blacklisted in 2020 by the US Department of Commerce, restricting its access to key US technologies. Walden no longer holds a stake in SMIC. Also of considerable note, in 2025, Walden founder and chairman Lip-Bu Tan, a prolific investor in China's semiconductor industry and throughout

Asia for many years, was named CEO of Intel, and is seen as the best chance of restoring the US chipmaker. Increasing scrutiny over his China ties led to a White House meeting with President Trump and a deal with the US government taking a 10 percent stake in Intel and Tan remaining as chief executive. A potential issue is Intel Capital's venture investment stakes in 43 China-based tech startups as of mid-2024, including AI and chip companies.[6]

Sequoia's Turn in DC

Sequoia Capital managing partner Roelof Botha and global chief policy officer Don Vieira received a letter from the Select Committee in October 2023, soon after the firm had announced a separation of operations into independent spheres, with HongShan running China. While noting that Sequoia's split "was a step in the right direction," the lawmakers raised questions about how the breakup "may affect flows of US capital and technological knowhow to foreign venture funds" and would "staunch future flows of American capital to problematic PRC companies." The lawmakers wrote that the split would "not prevent continued investment by US institutional investors into HongShan" and added that the Chinese fund would be able to "continue funneling US capital into PRC companies" and draw from "a large pool of American capital."

The committee further noted that about half of Sequoia Capital China limited partners are from the US, a drop from 60–70 percent for much of its existence, but still are the "single largest source of capital for Sequoia Capital China." The 2023 report's summary indicates that Sequoia Capital China informed the committee that its RMB funds don't have US limited partners.

The committee also questioned the prestigious Sand Hill Road firm about investment deals made with 40 Chinese semiconductor firms in the early 2020s and two AI companies, Eversec and 4Paradigm, that allegedly have links to the Chinese military. Gallagher and ranking member Raja Krishnamoorthi wrote that these deals "support the CCP's goals of ensuring technological supremacy and increasing the US dependence on the PRC in critical technologies."

Under further scrutiny were deals with sanctioned drone maker DJI over human rights abuses; facial recognition startup DeepGlint, blacklisted by the US Commerce Department in 2021; and AI startup 4Paradigm, cited for contracts with the (People's Liberation Army (PLA).[7]

Sequoia China's support and capital to ByteDance and TikTok did not escape notice, with the lawmakers noting these sites expose "millions of Americans to CCP surveillance and influence." The report spelled out that Sequoia and its China unit invested $1.4 billion in TikTok owner ByteDance starting in 2014, and added that venture capitalist Neil Shen was, and is, a board member.[8] (Representatives from US firms General Atlantic and Susquehanna International are also on the ByteDance board of directors.[9])

The findings made note, too, of Sequoia China's $30 million investment in Moonshot AI, a developer of a large-scale AI foundation model and creator of a smart assistant product Kimi Chat. The Select Committee called generative AI a national security risk.[10]

Silicon Valley Breaks Up with China

Not long ago, there was a two-way superhighway between Silicon Valley and China. Venture capitalists flew to and from Beijing, Shanghai, and Palo Alto frequently. Deals were made over WeChat, during weekend brunches, and in taxis caught in traffic jams. Competition for startup founders with a compelling pitch was fierce, for fear of missing out or what became known as FOMO.

Now, venture investors who once chased Chinese startups have slowed down, relocated offices, and stayed out of the spotlight. Some have feared retaliation or attention from Beijing, Washington—or both.

Many venture partners stopped giving media interviews and some scrubbed China references from their firm's websites. The chilling effect was real. The geopolitical climate had multiple Sand Hill Road venture capitalists fearing it wasn't "safe" to talk about investing in China. An often-repeated phrase began circulating among well-connected investors: "Those who know, don't talk. Those who talk, don't know."

> *"Those who know, don't talk. Those who talk, don't know."*
>
> **—Sand Hill Road** venture capitalists on dealings with China

The silence brought back recollections of several mysterious disappearances a few years ago related to Chinese government investigations such as when Alibaba's Jack Ma vanished from public life and influential tech dealmaker Bao Fan "went missing," for several months, in a broader government crackdown on corruption.[11]

For more than two decades, American investors played a key role in shaping China's tech rise. Now, the same Sand Hill Road venture capitalists who celebrated their billion-dollar exits were backing away from China. They had prided themselves on being in the forefront, but they began quietly unwinding their positions, selling off stakes in some of what had been China's most promising startups, closing China-focused funds, and separating China and US funds and operations. Meanwhile, limited partner investors in China VC funds were scrambling to get assurances that their cash would not go into companies that violated the rules. While US VC firms are not legally forced to divest from Chinese investments overall, they face growing political pressure and more restrictions that has reshaped their dealmaking.

After years of tackling China and reaping the rewards, what mattered now was how to shift strategy or cut ties with their Chinese operations. A clear and urgent reason was the US government's scrutiny and limits on American venture investing in China's emerging tech companies.

In the venture funding world, change was dramatic. Chinese tech titans like Baidu, Alibaba, and Tencent had all received financing from the US and foreign investors in the late 1990s and early 2000s. The enviable results of these investments was a powerful draw for Sand Hill Road.[12]

By 2018, China and US venture funding was almost on par: China at $105 billion; US at $118 billion. But a large gap developed within a few years as China fell way behind while the US kept soaring.

China's venture collapse wasn't triggered by a single event but by a perfect storm, caused by COVID-19 lockdowns, Beijing's regulatory hammer, the real estate market collapse, and the US–China geopolitical standoff.

By 2024, the tracking statistics told a stark story:[13]

- The number of China-focused venture funds sunk from 993 in 2020 to just 44 in 2024.
- Venture funding in China plummeted from RMB 91.4 billion to RMB 5.8 billion—a staggering 94 percent decline.
- US dollar investments into China-focused funds dried up, reaching only $45.8 billion—less than half of previous years.
- US-backed venture capital in China dropped sharply to 116 deals totaling $3.93 billion in 2023, the lowest annual level in a decade.[14]

It wasn't just about the money. The spirit of China's venture boom disappeared, too.

A veteran Silicon Valley investor in China who spent two weeks bouncing around five Chinese tech hubs didn't mince words: "It's dismal. Local governments play a dominant role in funding but demand guaranteed returns—that's antithetical to true venture capital. It's pretty depressing after participating in the venture excitement around 2003."

Beijing Takes Control of Venture Capital

As the US scrutiny of venture investing in China intensified, pressure was also building from the Chinese government on its tech titan investors. For years, China's startup ecosystem thrived on ambitious founders, deep-pocketed investors, and a relentless drive to compete. It worked—until government got involved.

In China, the freewheeling, risk-taking culture that had defined China's tech boom was replaced by the heavy hand of the state. Two-thirds of China's VC funding today now comes from state-backed entities—governmental funds, provincial banks, and politically connected firms.[15]

This shift toward government control left many American venture capitalists uneasy and uncertain about their future. Some of the best-known Silicon Valley investors in China faced the changing reality and left. For years, US venture capitalists had traveled to China several times a year, cutting deals and scouting talent. Now, after making a fortune in China, they settled in Singapore or California and rarely, if ever, went to mainland China—although they missed the frenzied days of dealmaking in Beijing and Shanghai.

Firms popped up that helped US VC firms offload their Chinese portfolio companies through secondary sales. Silicon Valley–based former ZhenFund venture partner and eBay tech exec Wei Jiang established CatchLight Capital Partners in 2020 and raised funds to acquire US portfolios from Chinese VC firms that were winding down assets. A scramble was also underway at US VC firms investing in China to separate out data for fund management and capital from limited partnership (LP) investors, such as pension funds.[16]

In the summer of 2024, a party hosted by former Alibaba CEO and private equity investor David Wei at his Silicon Valley mansion drew tech investors and entrepreneurs from China. "They were dying to get involved in Silicon Valley and were depressed and unhappy about being excluded because they were not US citizens," a partner of a major Sand Hill Road firm told me. The scene was described as something out of *The Great Gatsby*, the Roaring Twenties parties for the ultra-wealthy on Long Island's North Shore.

Hybrid funds, which combine private capital with state industrial objectives, have now become more dominant, prioritizing investment in emerging technologies such as quantum computing, AI, robotics, and high-end chips. But they may not be so effective. A study of so-called government guidance funds (GGFs) found that, from 2005 to 2021, only 26 percent raised their target capital size and two-thirds (particularly those in the northeastern rust belt of China) did not make a single investment.[17]

More state funding of tech startups is coming. China has recently announced a fund of 1 trillion ($138 billion) to grow AI, quantum computing, robotics, and other emerging technologies critical to the economy. The fund is structured as a 20-year partnership with state-backed entities and private capital.

"What's happening now is that the RMB money has adopted a higher-risk profile than it had 20 years ago. It's more willing to go into earlier stage tech companies," observed Gary Rieschel of Qiming Ventures, a pioneer of Chinese VC, in an interview with me. He continued:

> The first RMB funds wanted nothing to do with hard-core technology risk. The Chinese government has continued to be conflicted in terms of its real risk appetite in a lot of ventures. They don't want to lose any money so they're partnering with firms like Qiming and HongShan to manage funds on their behalf. They're trying to leverage some of the expertise that the funds have.

Rieschel pointed out that the Chinese government's results have been mixed. "If you just look at semiconductors, they blew up about $50 billion. It has not been a glorious outcome of innovation investing by the government, at least in semiconductors." He was referring to several government-subsidized and funded multibillion-dollar chip foundries that failed in China after corruption scandals, and, as Rieschel worded it, "the sheer capital intensity in building chips."

Where are Your Unicorns?

Venture capital, by nature, thrives on risk, speed, and a willingness to fail. But China's new top-down system demanded predictability, guaranteed returns, and compliance.

One veteran venture capitalist—who had backed some of China's most successful startups—recounted a tense meeting with Chinese government officials in late 2023.

"They kept asking: 'Where are your unicorns [privately held startups valued at over $1 billion]?'" he told me. "I wanted to say, 'That's not how this works. Unicorns don't appear just because you demand them.'"

When evaluating potential deals in China, "you had to decide if an investment was being made for political reasons or for commercial reasons," said longtime US–Asian investor Stephen Markscheid, managing principal at family office investment firm Aerion Capital in Chicago.

Yet, despite the challenges, China's track record of creating unicorns has held up (see Table 5.1). The country still ranked second only to the US in the number of unicorns:[18]

Table 5.1

Number of unicorns by top 10 global cities (2024)

City	Number
San Francisco	190
New York	133
Beijing	78
Shanghai	65
London	45
Shenzhen	34
Bangalore	32
Paris	25
Guangzhou	24
Hangzhou	24

Source: Hurun Report, CVinfo, Gobi Partners

- Beijing alone housed 78 unicorns.
- Shanghai had 65.
- Shenzhen, Guangzhou, and Hangzhou together added another 82.
- ByteDance, the most valuable of them all, was worth $300 billion—second to SpaceX—although another more recent report put ByteDance at third, behind OpenAI.[19]
- Bright spots have appeared, particularly in AI, such as a $1 billion funding of Moonshot AI in 2024.

Startups Go Hungry

For China's entrepreneurs, raising capital was no longer about investors willing to bet on their bold ideas and knack for moving fast. Within a few short years, they were squeezed out of funding. Startups in sectors deemed national security risks by the US government—AI, semiconductors, quantum computing—were locked out of American capital. Seeking funding from China's provincial governments wasn't a good alternative to experienced Sand Hill Road investors. The numbers painted a stark picture:

- In 2018, a record 51,000 new venture-backed startups were founded in China.
- By 2023, that number had plummeted to just 1,200.[20]
- Many founders, unable to secure fresh investment, were forced to shut down or pivot.
- The chill extended to IPOs. For years, an IPO on the New York Stock Exchange or Nasdaq was the ultimate

trophy for a Chinese entrepreneur and a way to cash out after the hard work in starting up. The logic was simple: US markets provide deeper pools of capital, higher valuations, and global prestige. Now that exit route was full of hurdles:

- IPOs of Chinese companies in New York slowed significantly in 2022 and onward.[21]
- In 2022, Chinese ride-hailing giant Didi was forced to delist from the New York Stock Exchange, in part due to Beijing's escalating data security concerns.
- By 2023, in the wake of volatile financial markets, China's regulators paused all domestic IPO approvals for nearly 18 months, stalling growth for thousands of startups.
- In 2024, IPOs on Mainland China exchanges totaled just 101, down 75 percent from two years earlier.[22]

The dry spell in China was captured in a global survey by investment management firm Adams Street Partners. It not too surprisingly found that fewer limited partner investors (which back VC and private equity funds) see compelling private market opportunities in China while interest in Emerging Asia investments has picked up.[23]

Gary Rieschel, a leading voice on China's innovation economy, has been through boom times and downturns, and he's frustrated by the limit on IPOs in China:

> Government intervention with IPOs has not been a market-oriented, entrepreneurial-oriented intervention. It's been very much about "here's something we can control" and that doesn't work. When you turn off the

> spigot for 12 to 24 months on the capital, on the ability to take companies public in a market, that's going to put a pretty big chill on the entire system, not just any particular company or market.

The crunch has been painful for startups and their investors. To scramble for financial returns, some venture capitalists have demanded that founders return money due to failure to scale up their startups to an IPO or mergers and acquisitions deal. These "redemptions" nearly tripled to 641 in 2023.[24] Other firms required founders to assume personal liability for investments.[25]

Now, it was no longer about who could scale up the fastest. It was about who could adapt and survive.

In a widely read post on LinkedIn in 2024, Robert Wu, CEO of Shanghai data company BigOne Lab, sparked a mini storm about the near death of China's VC market and the "dire consequences" it would have on the industry ecosystem.[26]

The Buzz about "Hard Tech"

For nearly two decades, China's biggest startup successes had been in consumer tech. Apps like WeChat, TikTok (Douyin), and Meituan reshaped everyday life, fueled by venture money that chased fast growth and quick exits.

Now that model was dead—the new buzzword? "Hard tech."

Instead of social media and e-commerce, China's government made its priorities clear that the future belonged to sectors that could strengthen the nation's industrialization: semiconductors, AI, autonomous driving, and robotics.

Now, large new funds were yuan-denominated and focused on Beijing's "Little Giants" initiative—small, highly specialized startups that the government believed could become "Manufacturing Champions."[27] A feeder was China's STAR market, a Nasdaq-style exchange for China's smaller innovative tech enterprises that started in 2019 and which, within two years, saw 350 listings, primarily those closely aligned with national industrial policies —and considered "still puny" compared to Shanghai and Shenzhen exchanges.[28]

Meanwhile, along Sand Hill Road, the impact of the crackdown on China venture investing was becoming clear.

Sand Hill Road VC Firms Investing in China Get a New Profile: A Look at the Major Players and How They Restructured

Sequoia has been regarded as the prestige player along Silicon Valley, and few venture capitalists have been as prominent as top-performing investor Neil Shen (b. 1967). Shen grew up in Shanghai and obtained a bachelor's degree from Shanghai Jiao Tong University then a master's degree from the Yale School of Management. He serves on the university's Greater China Board of Advisors, and a courtyard is named after him on campus in New Haven. Shen resides in Hong Kong and reportedly has recently obtained permanent residency in Singapore. I've known Shen since 2005 when Sequoia China was first set up; he's also an entrepreneur and a cofounder of two Chinese startups—online travel portal *Trip.com* and Homeinns Hotel Group.

In 2024, as a new chapter began for dealmaking in China, the separated Chinese venture firm HongShan proceeded to raise a RMB18 billion ($2.5 billion) fund that gave the firm broader scope for investments in key sectors.[29] HongShan also invested more in two Chinese portfolio companies, fast-growing social media sensation Xiaohongshu (or Little Red Book) and ByteDance, from a $9 billion fund that was raised in 2022. Simultaneously, HongShan, or HSG (as it became known), began expanding globally, opening offices in Singapore, London, and Tokyo. Several of its portfolio companies also set up a presence in Singapore, distant from China.

Notably Not GGV

Along that Sand Hill Road stretch next to Stanford University, GGV Capital—like Sequoia Capital before it—also split into two distinct firms. In Silicon Valley, GGV was branded Notable Capital, distanced from Chinese investments. Hans Tung, who has continued to be a star performer despite the break in his former forte of cross-border US–China deals, stopped making any new investments in China several years ago and is today investing in AI and fintech startups in the US.

In Singapore, a new entity was named Granite Asia, run by partners and perennial achievers Jenny Lee and Jixun Foo. Granite Asia has broadened its focus to Southeast Asia and Japan and recently invested $60 million in a US-based "AI-data foundry" that's exploring expansion to Asia. The firm also has expanded into private credit and a new fund securing loans for mid-sized enterprises in Asia. Venturing a bit from core tech, Granite Asia co-funded Supermom, a Singapore-based, AI-driven personal care platform designed for mothers. As for the firm's existing RMB funds, they are being managed by Eric Xu under a separate Chinese entity, Jiyuan Capital.[30]

The Waves Impact DCM

Along that same Sand Hill Road is DCM, a Silicon Valley–anchored investor in the US and Asia. In an interview for my first China book, *Silicon Dragon*, in 2008, cofounder David Chao predicted that China would see the likes of Steve Jobs. That largely came about. Think Lei Jun, the visionary founder of smartphone, and consumer electronics and electric vehicle maker Xiaomi.

DCM quickly ascended the ranks of elite Sand Hill Road firms investing in China as well as Japan and the US. But geopolitical headwinds prompted recalibration. In late 2024, partner Osuke Honda spun off a new $120 million fund to invest mainly in Japanese startups.

DCM began shifting away from Mainland China, a high-performing market that has represented one-third of its deals, led by veteran investor and entrepreneur Hurst Lin, a cofounder of China's first internet portal, SINA.

Lin has aced the *Forbes* list of top 100 VCS 10 times. To his credit are several notable hits from the earlier, go-go era: online retailer VIPShop and classified listings site 58.com. One of his best deals was short-form video site Kuaishou (China's version of Reels). Lin's $50 million investment swelled to a $16 billion stake following the IPO in 2021 in Hong Kong. Coinvestors were Tencent and top-ranked VCs 5Y Capital (rebranded from property tycoon Ronnie Chan's Morningside Capital) and Yuri Milner's firm DST Global. DCM is seeking to offload its remaining small stake in Kuaishou, and was anticipating several more Chinese IPOs soon, or when government approvals are given, Lin told me.

An out-of-the-box thinker who styles his red-colored hair in a punk style, Lin isn't afraid to voice his opinion. "Now, the funding in China is all in RMB. There's no upside incentive to run a VC. I think it's not going to go well. The power is with the politicians, not the VCs," he said, adding, "The sooner they admit their error, the sooner it will open up again."

In addition to hopping back and forth between Shanghai and Beijing, Lin now keeps a home in the San Francisco Bay Area, like many others from the Silicon Dragon era. He's joined the AI investing parade in the Valley, recently seeding two AI startups: coinvesting $10 million in FlowGPT, a Berkeley-founded startup with an open ecosystem for AI creators, and injecting $9 million into AI app developer BentoML and joining the board.

GSR in the Currents

In the heady days of 2005–8, Sonny Wu, a cofounder of GSR Ventures in Beijing, used to end our interviews by exclaiming, "The best is yet to come!" For a while, that was true. GSR rode the China tech wave, placing ambitious bets on AI, semiconductors, and next-generation consumer tech. But the firm found itself dealing with increased scrutiny and complex cross-border investments.

GSR, or Golden Sands River (a magical waterway in China that symbolizes innovation), carved its niche in deep-tech investments. From its start in 2004 as an affiliate of the Silicon Valley stalwart Mayfield, GSR leveraged a mix of capital, contacts, and local knowhow. The firm flourished, managing $3.7 billion in a mix of 12 US dollar and RMB funds from Silicon Valley, Beijing, and Singapore. It built an enviable track record with Alibaba-acquired food delivery service Ele.me, Nasdaq-listed online travel site QUNAR, and a record-breaking Hong Kong IPO, Horizon Robotics, an AI chip maker for autonomous vehicles. The firm was also an early investor in two ill-fated companies, ride-hailing service Didi and bike-sharing startup Ofo (see Chapter 7).

As one of the deepest and earliest tech investors in China, GSR has held an advantageous position for financial returns. But that became a negative.

GSR found itself under the microscope of Washington lawmakers for its push into Chinese AI and semiconductor companies and startups linked to China's surveillance. One was Moqi, a maker of fingerprint scanners with alleged ties to the PRC's Ministry of Public Security.

Initially, GSR was reluctant to provide information about its RMB investments, citing the PRC's data privacy laws, but after extensive negotiations, GSR did inform the Select Committee on the CCP that it had invested an approximate $15 million in five companies that the committee flagged.[31]

In early 2025, the firm, which has several US limited partners, followed the lead of several other prominent US–China venture firms. The team's China and US partnership split into two units. Its renamed Palo Alto–based firm Informed Ventures (taking a cue, perhaps, from GGV's Notable Capital in the US) is investing $200 million from an existing capital pool, chiefly in digital healthcare startups—a stronghold.

In a further separation from China, GSR Ventures has increased its presence in East Asia. In 2022, GSR Ventures hired Singaporean-born Yale and Harvard graduate David Yin as a partner to scout for potential investments in the region from a Singapore base. The firm has inked several investments in the Lion City including digital ID service Advance.AI, online health and wellness retailer EVO Commerce, and B2B global payments facilitator NIUM. Managing director Allen Zhu, long recognized as one of the top 100 venture capitalists globally by *Forbes*, now lists Singapore as his residence while keeping a keen eye on China's latest AI breakthroughs such as DeepSeek.[32]

The AI Maestro's Calculated Bet

Then there's Kai-Fu Lee (b. 1961), a former Google China president turned venture capitalist who is the face of China's AI revolution. When we first met in 2006, he was running Google China, competing with China's Baidu search contender. After Google withdrew from the Chinese market in 2009, he forged his own path, founding Beijing-based Sinovation Ventures and amassing $3 billion in assets across 10 US dollar and RMB funds that backed some of the country's most promising startups. But, in 2019, he doubled down on China, shuttering the firm's Silicon Valley office, and sold off his firm's American holdings in 2021—moves that now seem prescient.

Despite pandemic-era restrictions when China was often in lockdown, Lee secured $200 million toward a fifth fund in 2022. He mined three IPOs in 2024: self-driving startup WeRide on Nasdaq, AI solutions provider 4Paradigm on HKSE, and automated forklift manufacturer EP Equipment, in Shanghai. Meanwhile, his own AI startup, 01.AI, co-funded with Alibaba, introduced an AI-powered search tool, BeaGo, working with images, not words.

His commitment to China has drawn both admiration and skepticism, though some experts wonder if he has taken too big a risk and chosen the wrong camp.[33]

Lightspeed: A Calculated Detachment

While some firms have struggled to navigate the US–China tech divide, Lightspeed Venture Partners has kept its China operations independent while maintaining the global brand. Its China unit invests exclusively in Mainland deals through affiliate Lightspeed China Partners, which broke off from the Silicon Valley anchor in 2012. That early separation has given Lightspeed China greater agility to navigate geopolitical headwinds and industry shifts. Led by founding partner James Mi, a former Google China M&A executive, the firm delivered blockbuster IPOs, including Meituan and Pinduoduo. In 2021, Lightspeed China raised $920 million to target climate tech, AI, and deep tech. Mi sees plenty of upside.

"China has become a true innovation hub for deep tech and climate tech," said Mi, speaking at a recent Asian venture forum held by the *Asian Venture Capital Journal* (AVCJ) in Hong Kong. "You can spend $35 million and build world-class businesses, and take them public. It's very attractive to us. Early-stage valuations for tech startups are the lowest we've seen in 10 years. It's an opportune time to invest more since valuations remain very attractive," he noted, especially for brand-new startups.

The decline of global limited partner interest and investment in Chinese funds has separated out the survivors like Lightspeed China. "There's a decline of global limited partner investment in China and a flight to quality, top funds that can continue to raise decent fund sizes," said Mi, a Princeton University master's graduate in electrical engineering who also has aced the *Forbes* list of top 100 venture capitalists.

As the US–China divide has widened, he sees opportunity in the rebalancing toward "China for China." He noted that renminbi-denominated funds now dwarf US dollar counterparts in China, and predicted more IPOs will be on China domestic exchanges than in New York. With both RMB and dollar funds, Lightspeed China has leverage at an opportune time.

Qiming's Strategic Adaptation

Few firms have adapted to China's shifting venture landscape as skillfully as Qiming Venture Partners, founded in 2006, and supersized to $9.5 billion in capital under management. Despite the recent uncertainties over US–China superpower tensions, Qiming has powered up, raising successively larger funds, the most recent in 2022 at $2.5 billion. Now, Qiming is raising its ninth US dollar and eighth RMB fund.

The firm's next flagship dollar fund for China will be "significantly smaller than the last fund, and the last fund was big," said co-founder Rieschel. "Virtually all the Chinese funds are raising smaller funds than they did two to three years ago. And that's a just a reflection of the geopolitical reality where a lot of US investors are no longer as excited about China because of geopolitics. And the bigger issue has been the liquidity for many firms in China has been poor," he said candidly.

One of the most tuned-in investors in China–US venture, Rieschel brings 35 years of experience in Silicon Valley, Japan, and China at SoftBank, Cisco, and three early China VC firms he helped to set up. A Harvard MBA, he's outspoken and transparent in influential circles about ongoing US–China tensions. I've known him for years as a wise and trusted source, and he's spoken at several of my Silicon Dragon VC and tech forums and appeared on my online show, *AskAVC*—as have others in this chapter.

"This is the first real slowdown China has seen since venture capital institutionalized in 2005," Rieschel relayed in his deep, booming voice. "The market is not used to anything, but up into the right in terms of size of funds and deployment of capital. So everyone feels like this is slowing down. Qiming is still doing 30-plus deals a year, so I view that as slower than the peak, but not at all what I would call slow."

"I think that the big change for everyone is that there was a lot of stupid money deployed back in the 2013 to 2020 era in some of the consumer models that wound up wasting a great deal of capital," he continued. "If you had a portfolio that was heavily exposed to that, and you were still deploying capital in the 2016–17 to 2020 timeframe, then you have a lot of work to do on that portfolio."

In 2016, Qiming "started to put more investment in core tech, semiconductor equipment, advanced manufacturing—much more core tech base than two cycles ago," Rieschel explained. "These kinds of deals take a "technically oriented entrepreneurial pool. Entrepreneurs from 2009 to 2019 can't easily pivot to doing real core tech."

The firm has evolved to investing in "hard tech"—semiconductors, AI, autonomous driving, and robotics—areas aligned with Beijing's national priorities. Qiming issued a 2023 press release from a .cn domain and featured cofounder Duane Kuang's Chinese name. The release, translated from Chinese to English, underscored that China's VC ecosystem is moving toward a stage of technological innovation, and noted that hard technology has become the main line of China's economic development and industrial transformation. The release described Qiming as an important connector between technological innovation and industrial upgrading and stated its investment goal of "hardcore innovative companies with high technical barriers and high industrial value."[34]

Qiming has scaled up its renminbi-denominated funds to invest more in China. From an initial RMB 250 million ($36.6 million) pool in 2010 with China's National Development and

Reform Commission to invest in Chinese biomedical startups, Qiming completed its seventh fund at RMB 6.5 billion ($900 million) in 2023, and is working toward the eighth RMB fund of about the same size.

"Over 90 percent of the venture capital money now being deployed in China is in RMB. If you're managing dollar funds as your only source of capital, you're not participating in a lot of the deals that are getting done," said Rieschel.

The New Normal

In addition to marquee investors Princeton, MIT, and Duke in the US, Qiming has pulled in capital from several China state-owned enterprises, insurance institutions, and government-backed and guided funds including China Development Bank Capital and Chinese investment bank and private equity investor CICC.

The firm's lean-in to China strategy has been working from successful deals earlier on with Chinese tech winners Xiaomi and Meituan to more recently, multiple IPOs of Chinese portfolio companies including humanoid robotics company UBTech on the Hong Kong Stock Exchange in 2023, autonomous driving startup WeRide on Nasdaq in 2024, and renewable energy company HyperStrong in 2025 on Shanghai's STAR Market.

Looking ahead, Qiming has been undergoing a generational transition. Managing partner Nisa Leung has recently departed after leading the firm's biotech investing since 2006, and backing dozens of startups in this booming sector, including Nasdaq-listed biopharmaceutical giant Zai Lab, coronavirus vaccine maker CanSino Biologics, and generative AI-powered drug developer Medicine.

A Victory Lap

Rieschel, who made a well-timed relocation to Seattle in 2016 after 11 years residing in Shanghai, still travels to China at least twice a year and oversees the firm's US healthcare investments through a separate fund. He also has gotten more involved in industry-leading positions such as chairing Asia Society Northern California and serving on the Atlantic Council's board of directors.

Years ago, Rieschel told me he would know when it was time to take "his victory lap." Qiming's trajectory suggests he has earned it. His firm Qiming, true to its name meaning "to enlighten and inspire," has played a defining role in China's evolving venture market.

For Qiming and other firms that were well placed along Sand Hill Road and Beijing hotspots and were pioneers in China tech investing, the best days were great, they may not be over yet, but success in China is more uncertain and challenging than ever.

part three

AN EXPLORATION OF CHINA'S GAIN IN THE TECH SECTORS THAT MATTER MOST

CHAPTER 6

A CHINA—US FACE-OFF IN ARTIFICIAL INTELLIGENCE

China lags OpenAI in advanced artificial intelligence (AI) but is catching up quickly, as Hangzhou-based startup DeepSeek suddenly demonstrated. Chinese tech titans have also entered the fray with their own large language models.

In early 2025, the sudden rise of Chinese AI startup DeepSeek rattled Silicon Valley's high-tech sector. This challenger showed up the Microsoft-backed sensation OpenAI for efficiency and some performance benchmarks. It wasn't just a breakthrough. It was a wakeup call. And it provoked fear that China was getting ahead faster than most in the US had thought.

DeepSeek's leap forward sharpened concerns in the ongoing US–China tech rivalry. Washington lawmakers raised issues about whether and how DeepSeek used restricted Nvidia chips to power its AI models, and called DeepSeek a national security threat for censorship, foreign control, and data risks.[1]

In the Silicon Valleys of the US, DeepSeek's breakthrough sent a signal about China's technological sophistication and prospects that it could catch up with—or surpass—the US in shaping the future of AI. OpenAI CEO Sam Altman called DeepSeek an "impressive model." Microsoft's Satya Nardella went even further, admitting it was the first system he'd seen that could match up to OpenAI. Leading venture capitalist Marc Andreessen likened the launch of DeepSeek's new model to AI's "Sputnik moment"—the Soviet Union's 1957 satellite launch and earth orbit that spurred the space race. Nvidia's CEO, Jensen Huang, whose chips are the center of the geopolitical tug-of-war, said he believes Chinese AI scientists are "not Chinese AI researchers, they're world-class AI researchers."

These comments framed China not as a fast follower but a peer or rival. Before DeepSeek, it was widely considered that China was behind the US in this advanced AI market shaped by tech titans Microsoft, Google, Amazon, and well-financed startups. DeepSeek helped to close that gap.

Now, AI investors put DeepSeek in the same grouping as American leaders. The new investor acronym replacing FAANG is MANGO—or Microsoft, Anthropic, Nvidia, Google, DeepMind, and OpenAI.[2]

None other than Mary Meeker, a Silicon Valley investor and trendspotter well known for her annual report on tech trends, found that, while the US ranks number one with nearly 150 large-scale AI systems, China is catching up with just over 100. This means the world will be relying on US or Chinese AI technologies, raising concerns about data privacy, ethical alignment, and geopolitical leverage. It's also why the US has limited the sale of AI chips to Chinese companies.[3]

Until DeepSeek burst onto the scene, the consensus among Western analysts was that China lagged in the AI race.

The field has been largely dominated by American giants—Microsoft, Google, Amazon—and turbocharged by billion-dollar upstarts like Anthropic. What China lacked was its own OpenAI: a flagship that could compete with Silicon Valley's best. DeepSeek's entry helped China start to catch up with the US on the AI frontier. The US lead over China has narrowed from about nine months to just a *few weeks*, said AI entrepreneur Frank Yu, a former Microsoft China Research manager in Beijing. "Even in China, I think they were surprised that this little company—essentially a hedge fund that has GPUs [graphics processing units] and experience in quant trading—was able to build this model so quickly."

In a telling moment that underscored how far DeepSeek's advances and how high the stakes had risen, its founder, Liang Wenfeng, was seated in the front row of the Great Hall of the People, alongside tech luminaries Jack Ma of Alibaba and Pony Ma of Tencent. The occasion was a high-profile symposium convened by President Xi in early 2025, aimed at encouraging tech innovation and entrepreneurial ambition across the nation. Liang's prominent position was a signal about a new wave of AI pioneers that could shape China's role in a tech superpower race. Already, AI was transforming sectors, increasing productivity and automating manufacturing, streamlining office administrative tasks, guiding autonomous vehicles, and enhancing patient care.

Few voices have been more prescient about China's potential in AI than Kai-Fu Lee. An AI investor, former executive at Google and Microsoft, and the author of *AI Superpowers*, Lee has been at the crossroads of Silicon Valley and Beijing for over three decades. Early on, he argued that China "was the only true national counterweight to the US in this important technology."[4] Some in the West dismissed this notion. But DeepSeek's rise gave new weight to his long-held view.

Lee has often pointed out that, in this current age, data is today what oil was yesterday. And China, with its vast population, and ubiquitous mobile and digital systems, has an advantage with more data to fuel AI systems. He contends that China also benefits from having "a better set, a larger set of implementers or good AI engineers who get the work done, who make the algorithms run fast, and connect to business logic." It's a culture of pragmatism and speed. "The West," he has said, "needs to revise its view of Chinese technology companies being copycats of Western products, and acknowledge that, in fact, in some categories, Chinese tech is best-in-class."[5]

When I met with Kai-Fu for a fireside chat at my Silicon Dragon event at the San Francisco Yacht Club in 2019, his outlook was characteristically bold. He predicted that the impact of AI would arrive faster than most people realized. Yet not even Lee, with years of experience in the tech ecosystem, could have foreseen that a Chinese startup—not one spun out of Baidu, Alibaba, or Tencent, but one from a quantitative hedge fund in Hangzhou—would so quickly shake up the AI world. It was a reminder that a next leap in AI might just as easily come from China as from Silicon Valley.

And it did soon. While chatbots or AI software that simulate conversations with users through text or speech have been commonplace since the 2010s, a major development came in the early 2020s—a groundbreaking advance in AI technologies with large language models (LLMs) and OpenAI's ChatGPT that can generate content based on search prompts. Wanting in on the excitement over Open AI and its ChatGPT, and aiming to be a world leader, China has jumpstarted more than 250 generative AI companies, several of them like DeepSeek that could emerge as champions.[6]

DeepSeek Sinks In

The emergence of DeepSeek from mathematics whiz Liang Wenfeng and his hedge fund, High-Flyer, has marked a turning point and created a whole new period of excitement. Released in January 2025, DeepSeek's technology was regarded as cutting-edge for using reinforcement learning and breaking down complexities into steps, a process akin to thinking out loud before coming up with a final answer. DeepSeek's open-source AI platform gave access for researchers and developers to explore its reasoning model (R1), which has spurred more Chinese companies, including Baidu and Alibaba, to build using the same approach. Remarkably, DeepSeek was trained using $5.6 million in computing power—a fraction of the $100 million typically required by US rivals.

> *"We're going to see a lot of other DeepSeeks."*
>
> **—Frank Yu,**
> AI entrepreneur and researcher

DeepSeek's origins and quick start exemplifies the ingenuity of hardworking Chinese tech entrepreneurs. It was a step forward for China entrepreneurship, known for optimizing and iterating efficiently rather than inventing. "DeepSeek found a way to develop something equivalent to OpenAI but faster and cheaper," said tech entrepreneur Frank Yu, who worked in Beijing for 17 years before returning to New York. "That forced everyone in the US to recalculate the formula for an AI company. Now that DeepSeek has released how to duplicate it, we're going to see a lot of other DeepSeeks not just in China, but in the US, Europe, and Middle East." (By the way, some of the Chinese models support conversations in English and can be easy to access even without a Chinese phone number.[7]) Yu predicted that "the gains will go to not just other startups, but also to OpenAI and Google, and other major companies. They're going to be using that technology to make themselves cheaper too."

Protecting its treasure, DeepSeek advised employees not to travel overseas to safeguard confidential information and intellectual property, and told headhunters not to approach staff.[8] DeepSeek also hired more Chinese engineers, who are choosing to stay in China rather than look to Silicon Valley for opportunities.

DeepSeek Rattles the Valley

The impact of DeepSeek was immediate on Wall Street, Washington, DC, and, perhaps most of all, Silicon Valley. In a significant development, DeepSeek proved that China could continue to be a contender without Silicon Valley money.

Money to Chinese AI startups from Sand Hill Road had stopped flowing after a series of regulations blocked investment. A trigger was a Georgetown University report in early 2023 about US venture capital (VC) investment in Chinese AI startups, which outlined the extent of transactions, named the top 10 US VC firms, and underscored potential risks. The report, from the university's Center for Security and Emerging Technology, noted that US investors were involved in 37 percent of the $110 billion raised by all Chinese AI companies from 2015 to 2021. The authors recommended increased screening of deals and mechanisms to restrict investment in privately held Chinese companies on the US Department of Commerce entity list and on the Defense Department's tally of companies linked to China's military-industrial complex.[9] In January 2025, the US Treasury Department implemented

President Biden's 2023 executive order to regulate US investment into AI, quantum computing, and semiconductor companies in countries posing national security risks. Now, many Silicon Valley firms have distanced US funds from China and are seeking to sell Chinese portfolio companies.

More limits on Chinese AI have followed. In response to the White House considering policies to maintain US leadership in AI, OpenAI's vice president of global affairs Chris Lehane submitted a proposal in March 2025 that described DeepSeek as state controlled and subsidized, and recommended that the US government ban its models and others produced by the PRC.[10] By late March, several states and federal agencies blocked DeepSeek on government devices and echoed earlier privacy and security concerns that data Chinese startups collect in the US is stored in China. The White House and Congress have been considering broader measures banning DeepSeek's use.[11]

On Wall Street, DeepSeek triggered a sell-off of AI giant Nvidia's stock, which lost nearly $600 billion in value. Concerns mounted over whether DeepSeek's increased efficiency would shake up Silicon Valley's love affair with generative AI startups. Venture investors, eager for the next new thing, had funded generative AI (genAI) newcomers at a level not seen since the dotcom boom of the late 1990s. And startups were seeking to scale up fast and go public:[12]

- Global AI venture investment nearly doubled to $100.4 billion (or more[13]) across 4,505 deals in 2024.[14] Nearly one-third of all VC funding went to this sector.
- Out of 72 new unicorns in 2024, nearly half were for AI companies.[15] And five Chinese generative AI companies were funded at unicorn levels as 2025 began.[16]

With DeepSeek's arrival, Silicon Valley investors began rethinking valuations to back new AI companies. In the GenAI rush of 2023 and 2024, Microsoft had invested $13 billion in OpenAI, while Amazon poured $8 billion into Anthropic, the maker of chatbot Claude, OpenAI's biggest rival. Venture firm Andreessen Horowitz inked 44 deals in AI-related startups globally, closely followed by Lightspeed Venture Partners. Elon Musk's xAI picked up a $6 billion investment, valued at $50 billion.[17]

Now with China's DeepSeek beating the Valley on costs and taking no venture capital, tech investors in the Bay Area got investor remorse—did they pay too much? Venture capitalist Umesh Padval, a partner at Thomvest Ventures, outlined that DeepSeek could be bad news for foundational models that raised large venture capital amounts but noted its efficiency could also lead to increased adoption and faster development cycles.[18]

Money and talent have been pouring into AI, with the US and China leading the charge as the key contenders. Experts have predicted the global AI market will rise 29 percent annually from $294 billion in 2025 to an estimated $1.77 trillion by 2032. GenAI is on an even steeper trajectory, projected to surge 39.6 percent annually, from $67.18 billion to nearly $968 billion by 2032.[19]

China's R&D Surge in AI

China stacks up well in important measures of advanced AI. China generated almost half of the world's top AI researchers, up from one-third three years ago, according to think tank MarcoPolo, run by the Paulson Institute.[20] Additionally, some of China's models are now outperforming their US counterparts on bilingual benchmarks, noted the Information Technology and Innovation Foundation.[21]

In R&D, China currently leads the world in the volume of AI research publications, while the US maintains an advantage in citation impact and private sector engagement.

China is also the global leader in genAI patent filings, with 38,000 applications between 2014 and 2023. The US follows with 6,276, while South Korea, Japan, and India round out the top five (see Table 6.1). According to the World Intellectual Property Organization, genAI patents have grown rapidly to represent 6 percent of all patent filings worldwide. Remarkably, six of the top ten companies behind these patents are headquartered in China (see Table 6.2).[22]

China's AI Central Planning

China's strong position in AI stems from a combination of state-backed financial support, university-led research, and AI innovation hubs. Abundant data for training AI and widespread adoption of the technology in industry and digital services

Table 6.1

Top countries filing for generative AI patents

China	38,210
US	6,276
Republic of Korea	4,155
Japan	3,409
India	1,350

Source: WIPO, *Patent Landscape Report—Generative Artificial Intelligence*, 2024

Table 6.2

Top 10 patent filers for generative AI

Tencent	2,074
Ping An Insurance	1,564
Baidu	1,234
Chinese Academy of Sciences	607
IBM	601
Alibaba Group	571
Samsung Electronics	468
Alphabet	443
ByteDance	418
Microsoft	377

Source: WIPO, *Patent Landscape Report—Generative Artificial Intelligence*, 2024

also have been spurs. Progress reflects President Xi's broader vision of building "new quality productive forces"—a policy of long-term economic growth through technological and industrial innovation and leveraging AI, big data, and other cutting-edge technologies.

As early as 2017, China laid out a plan to become the global leader in AI by 2030. Armed with a deepening pool of well-trained technical talent, that strong government backing, and a vast reservoir of data, China began climbing the AI innovation ladder and became a rival to the US.

The US, meanwhile, laid out its own AI national strategy in 2019. During his first term, President Trump launched the "American AI Initiative," directing federal agencies to prioritize AI investments and research. By 2025, the plan expanded to an AI Action Plan aimed at safeguarding US leadership in AI.

Some $500 billion of private sector funding was announced by OpenAI, Softbank, and Oracle for AI infrastructure. These plans signaled that Washington and Silicon Valley were united in this consequential technology race.

Which country wins depends on smarts, money, and willpower. And the US definitely has the upper hand. "Chinese companies are very good at applying AI and developing models but OpenAI and Google are the benchmarks," tech adviser and consultant Paul Triolo said.

The US–China AI race is far from over, however. New developments happen almost daily. One of the latest is Apple turning to Alibaba for AI features on its smartphones sold in China, its second-largest market. The deal, announced in early 2025, has raised fresh concerns in Washington over censorship, data sharing, and competitive intelligence.[23]

"Apple is sort of caught in this situation where they're going to get criticized for using Chinese AI models on their phones, but to compete in China in the advanced smartphone space, they're going to have to have more AI capabilities," said Triolo. The big issue for Apple is if they can't figure out a way to make sure they can deploy really good Chinese AI models as part of Apple Intelligence into their smartphones, then their competitiveness could erode over time." He added: "Samsung is working with Baidu and has deployed its Ernie Bot models on their handsets. Samsung hasn't run into the same controversy as Apple."

China's tech startups Baidu, Alibaba, and Tencent as well as Chinese AI startups like Moonshot AI and Zhipu AI—both backed by Alibaba—are aggressively pursuing the generative AI frontier. Alibaba is investing $53 billion over the next three years in artificial general intelligence (AGI) but is dwarfed by Microsoft's $80 billion in 2025 and spending by AWS, Meta, and Google. OpenAI has cut off access of its services to China since mid-2024.

Alibaba is aiming high in AGI with its Qwen family of LLMs including the recently released Qwen 3, geared for businesses with multiple languages and capable of complex reasoning as well as searches for quick answers. Early on, Baidu debuted its flagship chatbot, Ernie Bot, as a rival OpenAI's ChatGPT. Baidu also has been a pioneer in AI-driven transportation with its Apollo Go robotaxi service in China. Tencent launched its model Hunyuan, positioned for gaming and social media platforms.

China AI Travels Well

In China, AI is seemingly everywhere. Land in Beijing, check in at passport control with facial recognition and fingerprint scans, then use an app to hail a Didi self-driving vehicle to ride on the airport highway equipped with smart city devices that monitor traffic flows. At major intersections and public places across China, cameras with built-in facial recognition are recording footage at major intersections and public places to catch jaywalkers, break-ins, and shoplifting. Residents who don't follow the rules risk getting a bad social credit score for trustworthiness and are punished with limitations on traveling by plane, sending their children to private schools, or other benefits.

This tight watch has led to mixed reaction. From a Western, freedom-loving perspective, it's a negative that controls the public. From China's point of view and that of some tourists, too, these devices make the streets and subways in Beijing, Shanghai, and other urban centers seem safe.

What could be a limitation on China's gains is Chinese censorship of content. Domestic AI models must stick to the Communist Party's line and operate within China's Great Firewall of internet censorship. Strategy Risks' consultant Isaac Stone Fish in New York City observed:

> I think we have to remember that the internet in China, the training data in China is far inferior to the training data in the US, not only because more has been written in English, but much more importantly, because what is on the English internet is far less censored than what is on the Chinese internet, so China AI is reflecting something that's less a reflection of reality than the US internet. On the other hand, for images and videos, there's so much more surveillance data in China. Companies getting their hands on that can have really rich visual training libraries, and that also is much easier to translate globally, because it's much less language specific. Leading-edge visual apps are all over the world because they need a lot less translation.

A next frontier for China AI's push is the Global South—developing nations in Asia, Africa, and Latin America. China's growing AI footprint in these regions provides access to diverse languages, economies, and cultures—data that can be fed into AI models from China. By providing affordable AI-powered products and investments in digital infrastructure, China is aiming to be the dominant AI player in developing economies, columnist Hao Nan wrote in the *South China Morning Post*.[24] "This expansion is not just about technology—it is about reshaping the global digital order."

The Push against China's AI Brains

Starting about a decade ago, in the early days of China's AI development, Chinese tech giants Baidu, Alibaba, and Tencent powered up in this new sector and specialized in particular fields that build upon their strengths. Baidu integrated AI into its DuerOS line of smart household goods and Apollo self-driving technology. Alibaba relied on an AI cloud platform called CityBrain that crunches data and determines patterns for better urban planning while Alipay used facial recognition for payments. Tencent integrated rich media format such as face swapping effects and video chat filters into its social media, and was also investing in personalized medicine. Meanwhile, the Chinese government designated two startups to lead AI development: SenseTime for facial recognition and iFlyTek for voice technology.

SenseTime won my Silicon Dragon group's award for Chinese startup of the year in 2017, back when US–China cross-border venture and tech seemed unstoppable. That year, Chinese AI startups accounted for 48 percent of the $12.5 billion of financing in the sector, surpassing the US for the first time, according to market research firm CB Insights.

SenseTime was backed by several US firms including Qualcomm Ventures, IDG Capital, Silver Lake in addition to Alibaba as its largest shareholder and several other investors. The well-financed, Hong Kong university spin-out became one of China's most valuable startups. SenseTime developed camera surveillance technology that analyzes faces, car license plates, vehicle types, and events for public security in China. Its high-tech system verifies and identifies payments at staff-less checkouts, peer-to-peer lending, and phone unlocks. Its facial recognition technology lets passengers match personal ID cards with their tickets and luggage and reduce waiting times in long lines.

But the trajectory of these startups was cut short. SenseTime, iFlyTek, and several other Chinese AI firms were blacklisted in 2019 by the Department of Commerce for alleged involvement in high-tech surveillance and human rights abuses against Uyghur Muslims. The Commerce Department list is a red flag for US companies, restricting US business with the pinpointed Chinese firms.

SenseTime, China's most highly valued AI startup, was planning to raise $2 billion on a Hong Kong IPO in late 2019, but after landing on the Treasury Department's blacklist for investment, US investors were prevented from participating in the IPO. The offering was postponed by several weeks and then did raise $740 million. SenseTime has since moved into genAI technology, and its recent introduction of SenseNova is competing on Chinese-language strengths.

Likewise, Chinese facial recognition startup Megvii, founded by three Tsinghua graduates, was planning an IPO in Hong Kong in 2019 until the business was blacklisted. The firm has since broadened into AI solutions for city planning, retail, healthcare, and logistics management. Megvii was funded by several prominent cross-border VC firms including GGV Capital and Qiming Venture, as well as Kai-Fu Lee's Sinovation Ventures. GGV Capital has been seeking to divest from Megvii but has faced difficulties in part due to limited appetite for purchasing the shares.[25]

China's AI Boom

Well before upstart DeepSeek launched in 2025, Chinese tech titans showed they could compete in AI. In a surge of activity, China's tech giants introduced new LLMs and invested heavily. China's technology giants also invested in Chinese AI startups, alongside local VC firms and state-owned funds.

There's no clear AI leader yet in China like with OpenAI's dominance in the US, but none wanted to be left out:

- **Baidu** had an early mover advantage in its 2023 launch of Ernie Bot, a ChatGPT-like conversational AI chatbot which gained to more than 430 million users by 2024 and was moving to an open-source, free version in 2025. Baidu's upgraded versions included a reasoning model, Ernie X1, which Baidu touted as on par with DeepSeek R1 for performance at only half the price.[26] Baidu's $145 million fund is investing in Chinese AI-related startups including chip technology startup StarFive.
- **Alibaba** released Tongyi Qianwen, a ChatGPT-like model in English and Chinese in 2023. Following the DeepSeek entry, Alibaba launched an advanced AI LLM in its Qwen series, which can process text, video, images, and audio over laptops and smartphones while generating real-time text and natural speech responses.[27] Alibaba's new model is open-source (widely available for free), following a growing trend in China that could speed up AI adoption and innovation in China.[28] Alibaba secured a major win for its AI business in 2025 through a partnership with Apple to roll out AI integration for iPhones sold in China.[29]
- **Tencent** has benefitted from its Hunyuan AI LLMs and chatbots for businesses on WeChat. The Hunyuan series was first introduced in late 2023. Tencent unveiled a new AI reasoning model in March 2025 that has been called an equal to DeepSeek's R1 in performance and pricing.[30] Tencent has joined the AI spending race with a strategic focus on the technology. HSBC analysts projected that Tencent's AI capital expenditures could reach 90 billion yuan ($12.5 billion) in 2025.[31]

- **ByteDance** launched its first AI chatbot Doubao in 2023, which became a leader with 75 million users in China. The ByteDance family of AI products include: Jimeng, a text-to-video generator; Xinghui, which is used to generate images from text prompts; Kouzi, a tool for customer service chatbot development; and Maoxing, designed to provide emotional support to users. Some of the ByteDance apps are available overseas. For example, Doubao is known as Cici in international markets, while Jimeng is called Dreamina.[32] ByteDance allocated $20.6 billion for capital expenditures in 2025, and the bulk of that money is being spent on boosting its AI-related infrastructure such as data center resources and networking equipment.[33]

China's 4 AI Tigers

Tech clusters are forming around leading AI startups and their investors. Hangzhou is home to China's "six little dragons," or rapidly emerging tech startups that span AI, robotics, brain-computer interfaces, and gaming development. These startups here leverage Alibaba's startup culture, other innovative startups such as Unitree Robotics, and faculty and alumni of Zhejiang University.[34]

Similarly, Tsinghua University in Beijing has become the breeding ground for China's leading AI startups, including four of the country's "AI tigers," all founded by faculty and alumni:[35]

- **Zhipu AI**, founded in 2019, became a unicorn in 2024 and was added to the US entity list in 2025, prohibited from procuring US components and technologies without a special license. Now, it's aiming to go public on a Chinese stock exchange. Invested in by HongShan, Legend Capital, Alibaba, Tencent, and a host of other Chinese majors at $340 million in 2023, Zhipu AI pulled in an additional $137 million in 2025 from two state-backed investors in Hangzhou.

- **Baichuan AI**, founded by Wang Xiaochuan, former CEO of major Chinese search engine Sogu, recently pivoted to focus on AI healthcare. The Beijing-based startup raised $350 million in 2023 at a valuation past $1 billion.
- **Moonshot AI**, founded in 2023 by renowned AI researcher Yang Zhilin, builds LLMs that can handle long inputs of data and text. It's best known as the creator of Kimi, an advanced chatbot that can process up to 2 million Chinese characters in a single prompt, or a query a user enters. Moonshot attracted more than $1 billion in finance in 2024 that valued the startup at more than $2.5 billion, co-led by Alibaba and HongShan with several tech titans on board. Prior investment of $200 million came from HongShan and ZhenFund.
- **MiniMax**, founded in 2021 by a former vice president at Chinese AI company SenseTime, released a text-to-video generation tool that is considered a competitor to OpenAI's Sora. A unicorn, it's backed by Alibaba and Tencent and raised about $850 million by 2024. Its English-language app Talkie is one of America's more popular entertainment apps. Talkie lets users converse with digital approximations of Elon Musk, Taylor Swift, and even Trump.[36] Talkie has not been banned but did face a temporary removal for technical reasons in December 2024.

Several other Chinese upstarts are worth following closely:

- **Metaso**, an AI startup in Shanghai funded by Lightspeed's China affiliate that is modeled after Perplexity AI, provides conversational answers from web-based AI search.
- **Stepfun**, founded in 2023 by a former Microsoft Research Asia scientist in Beijing, is a contender thanks to its foundation models and backing from Tencent and the Shanghai government.
- **ModelBest**, one of the Tsinghua-originated AI startups, is focused on highly efficient, small language models.
- **Manus AI**, backed by US VC Benchmark alongside Tencent, HongShan Capital, and ZhenFund, has popped up with a powerful AI agent in a new area of GenAI based on agents or little programs that can plan and complete specific tasks automatically like rebooking flights. The investment by Benchmark is reportedly under review by the US Treasury Department over compliance with regulations restricting US investment in Chinese AI companies.

Wow, What a World!

Not to be left out, AI superpower Kai-Fu Lee ignited his own generative AI startup business, 01.AI, from his Beijing-based research lab of 200 people (many of them with PhDs, including his own from Carnegie Mellon). The lab had strategically stockpiled advanced chips early on for training and running large-scale models, before tighter US export restrictions prevented Chinese companies from getting access to more sophisticated Nvidia chips (not the less powerful ones that Nvidia later built specifically for Chinese customers).[37]

A venture capitalist and AI innovator with years of tech experience, Lee became the face of China's AI revolution. When he launched Sinovation Ventures in 2009, he bet that China could advance rapidly in AI. Lee has since raised more than $3 billion, fueling some of the country's most promising AI startups. I've followed his work for several years, visiting his office in Beijing and interviewing him on stage at Silicon Dragon events in Hong Kong and San Francisco. In 2024, I observed his team creating a stir with the launch of an AI-powered search tool, BeaGo, that displays images next to a single answer on mobile. Lee has posted several times about the app to his millions of social media followers, urging them to download and try it out.

AI entrepreneur Frank Yu, who was recommended to BeaGo by his mentor Kai-Fu Lee, gave it a good review, noting that "it promises to outshine Google and Perplexity by delivering one coherent, comprehensive answer to queries. If you're looking for a smarter way to search, definitely give BeaGo a try."

At an event held by the Economic Club of New York in 2024, it was fascinating to hear Lee talk about how he was working on importing his speeches, research papers, and books into a genAI robot. Presumably designed to be a Kai-Fu Lee lookalike with his full head of thick, black hair, this robot would travel around and give speeches whenever given the cue.

Wow, what a world! The US–China AI race is bound to intensify but who will win the AI superpower crown is an open question.

CHAPTER 7

A NOT-SO-SHARED ECONOMY

Startups in China's once-promising bike-sharing, coworking, and ride-hailing markets such as Mobike, Ucommune, and DiDi have slowed down in an overheated and highly regulated environment that saw some collapses like well-funded Ofo. Yet they showed the way for Lime, WeWork, and Uber.

During China's bike-sharing boom in 2017–18, the city streets were jammed with bicyclists, all pedaling fast to get to work and run errands. It brought me back to my first visit to the country in 1995, when the roads were full of bicycle riders. Back then, bikes were not a choice but a part of everyday life. The few automobiles that passed were black sedans, reserved for officials and dignitaries.

But now bikes were back—this time as symbols of a tech-fueled China. Digital technology transformed urban mobility as the fast, easy, and cool way to get around. Cyclists could tap a smartphone app to locate bikes and scan a QR code to unlock it, ride it, and then drop it at their destination, eliminating the need for docking stations. Payment was by digital wallet, which had become ubiquitous in China's leap into the mobile age. It was a fusion of tradition and technology that reflected a new era.

Popularized for bicycles, this collaborative model soon spread to offices, lodges, cars, and kitchens, and to experiments with shared umbrellas, mobile chargers, and basketballs. Sharing brought economic, communal, and environmental benefits—well suited for a large, urban population with more limited resources. The cost of ownership and maintenance was, in effect, collective and distributed by need. Digitally savvy Chinese consumers took to this flexible and affordable lifestyle option for travel, housing, eating, and working.

This became big business. At its peak in 2018, 600 million Chinese people used a shared service and made some $500 billion in transactions.[1] China embraced the sharing economy ahead of other nations that soon caught on to the idea. The Chinese government boosted the sharing economy as a national priority in 2015–16, and forecast growth by 2020 to 10 percent of the GDP, spurred in part by tax breaks.

Startups quickly emerged and took leadership positions, most notably Mobike in bike-sharing, DiDi Chuxing in ride-hailing, and Ucommune in coworking. I had followed these startups in China and tracked their milestones, from funding to expansion to potential IPOs and acquisitions. Their founders were among China's first tech entrepreneurs—impressive, hardworking, and up to the challenge. Their equivalents in the US were LimeBike, Uber, and WeWork. They all pedaled fast and furious.

But this new economy didn't quite live up to its hyped potential in China. Timing was partly to blame. The sharing economy was picking up about two years before the coronavirus pandemic of 2020–22. Lockdowns and travel restrictions meant going nowhere.

The sharing economy, once heralded as a transformative force, began to resemble a shrinking economy. An oversupply of products, reduced demand, high overhead costs, and cash-burning operations led to many flops. This was especially true for capital-intensive markets, like with bicycles. But others simply fell out of favor. Ghost or shared kitchens for meal ordering by mobile app from a central supplier were a lifeline for the restaurant industry during COVID-19 lockdowns, but this practice lost its appeal once in-person dining resumed.

While many of these ventures faltered, some digital-only services not only survived but thrived. Much like Zoom's ascent, China's platforms such as Alibaba's DingTalk and Tencent Meeting became essential tools for remote communications in education, healthcare, and many industries. E-commerce also flourished, with online ordering and contactless delivery becoming the norm.

Bike-Sharing Boom and Bust

The boom-and-bust cycle of China's bike-sharing business offered a lesson in the challenges of managing rapid growth in a changing economy. Fueled by substantial venture capital, nearly 60 startups deployed an estimated 18 million brightly colored bicycles across Chinese cities at the peak.[2]

I met and interviewed the founders of Ofo and Mobike, two of the hottest startups. Peking University student and first-time entrepreneur Dai Wei named his startup Ofo to resemble a rider on a bicycle and branded his bikes with canary yellow to make them stand out. Backed by Alibaba, Yuri Milner's DST Global, and several leading US–Chinese VC firms, he spread his Uber-like service for bikes to 150 cities across five countries and was geared up for 20 countries. Former automotive executive Joe Xia, the cofounder and chief technology officer of Mobike, spoke at my Silicon Dragon tech and venture event in Beijing in 2017 about scaling up the business in China by getting into related services and entering as many as 200 overseas cities. Mobike, funded by Tencent, Sequoia Capital, Qiming Ventures, and others, launched in Singapore, the UK, and Japan. Both founders chased the market opportunity in China first, then tapped overseas for growth. Meanwhile, the Chinese idea of bike-sharing that these startups first popularized in the Mainland was spreading. Several lookalike upstarts such as Silicon Valley–based LimeBike swung into action.

But this surge was not sustainable. Intense competition among too many bike-sharing startups spurred aggressive discounting and too-rapid expansion. Operational challenges, such as maintenance of vast fleets and vandalism and theft, further strained resources. As bikes were dropped haphazardly at the end of each ride, they blocked sidewalks and piled up in so-called "bike graveyards."[3] Customers were unable to get their deposits back, and cities grappled with the environmental problem of rusted, abandoned bikes, eventually taking them to hidden recycling facilities. Ultimately, bike-sharing startup Ofo burned through $2.2 billion before collapsing in 2019 in the frenzy of this supercompetitive market, one of China's crazier venture phases.[4]

Ofo founder Dai Wei was trying his entrepreneurial luck again by forming About Time Coffee, a tech-driven boba coffee chain in New York City. Mobike, pumped up with $900 million in venture money, has fared better. It was acquired by food services app Meituan for $2.7 billion in 2018, and was integrated into the new owner's broader platform for deliveries. Mobike cofounder Xia has moved on as CEO of JiDu Auto Company, a joint venture of search engine Baidu and auto producer Geely, working on developing autonomous electric vehicles.

It was amazing to see how quickly the bike-sharing market shifted. The challenges in China's roller-coaster economy—even for well-funded startups supported by China tech titans Alibaba and Tencent—were formidable.

Ucommune Challenges WeWork

Another story of unfulfilled promise in China's shared economy popped up in the coworking market. It involved Chinese startup Ucommune competing with WeWork in China. On a visit to Ucommune's flagship location in Beijing in 2018, I entered the space by facial recognition. Ucommune's founder Daqing Mao excitedly told me about his startup's evolution from a typical co-office space with free coffee, hot desks, and networking events into a technology platform. The office was outfitted with IoT technologies to connect desks, sensors for heat and light controls, and computerized cameras to track occupancy levels and usage. His concept of movable "intelligent technology tables" was being tested in Beijing to operate without any management present.

Ucommune expanded to more than 40 Chinese cities, acquired a rival, and was going for a New York Stock Exchange IPO in 2019. But following WeWork's failed public listing in 2019 and investor skepticism, Ucommune went public on

Nasdaq in 2020 through a special purpose acquisition company (SPAC). Since then, the coworking outfit has struggled with financial losses,[5] shifted to digital services, and transitioned to a franchise model, while cutting costs by closing several coworking spaces in China.

WeWork in China also rode the ups and downs of startup experiences in an emerging economy. In 2018, during the height of the action, my group Silicon Dragon held a well-attended tech innovation event in WeWork's trendy renovated space within a nineteenth-century Shanghai structure that had been an opium factory. Incredible to think of the large turnout we had for that event. Today, many tech stars and their investors in this arena are staying out of sight. Miranda Wang, the cofounder of one of China's top unicorns, Xiaohongshu ("Little Red Book"), spoke at that event as did several top-tier venture capitalists, including Chibo Tang of Gobi Partners and Helen Wong of Qiming Venture.[6]

After the scuttled IPO of WeWork in New York City in 2019, the parent company sold a majority stake of its Chinese operations for $200 million to Shanghai-based private equity firm TrustBridge Partners.[7] WeWork China became an independent operation in 2020, but the timing was unfortunate—the start of COVID-era lockdowns (which also paused—ended—my Silicon Dragon forums in Beijing and Shanghai, though not Hong Kong which have continued). WeWork's localized expansion plans were halted in 2021. Recovery has been tough. Although present in 12 cities throughout Greater China,[8] key locations such as Shanghai and Shenzhen remain low occupancy, and more than one-third of the spaces are empty. But demand for premium coworking has picked up in Hong Kong, where WeWork China has several locations.

The Rise and Fall of DiDi

Of all the contenders in China's burgeoning shared economy, ride-hailing giant DiDi stood out as the most promising. It was innovative and growing fast. But its decline was just as notable. DiDi ran into regulatory troubles, delisted from the New York Stock Exchange (NYSE) in 2022, and was fined $1.2 billion by the Chinese authorities for data privacy violations. While the pandemic played a role, the reasons went beyond COVID—tied up in regulatory pressures, strategic missteps, and missed diversification opportunities.

"DiDi became a symbol of everything regulators wanted to rein in—market dominance, data control, and global ambition unchecked by domestic oversight," said Kendra Schaefer, a partner at Trivium China, who specializes in Chinese tech policy.[9]

DiDi's startup story was rooted in bold ambition. Nowhere was that more visible than at its modern headquarters, an hour's ride from Beijing's Forbidden City in the high-tech zone Zhongguancun in the northwest of this sprawling megalopolis. You knew you'd arrived by the colorful DiDi taxi sculpture parked out front.

Bolstered by substantial subsidies, and the convenience of booking and paying by mobile app, DiDi's vehicles in Beijing and Shanghai became as common as yellow taxis in Manhattan. They also appealed to tourists and expatriates, with an English-language interface, DiDi EN, used by more than 2 million English speakers across 430 cities in China within two years.[10]

To those outside China, it was best known as the startup that outmaneuvered Uber in the Chinese market. Backed by Tencent, Alibaba, and SoftBank, and even a $1 billion investment from Apple, DiDi waged a fierce battle with Uber in China for market share—one that ended in 2016 when the

American ride-hailing service sold out to its Chinese rival in a deal worth $35 billion.

Uber had been burning through enormous sums with subsidized rides to chase DiDi, while also dealing with China's varied local and national regulations. By absorbing Uber and a domestic Chinese rival, Kuadi Dache, the year before, DiDi consolidated its grip on the country's China's large and rapidly growing ride-share market. During the peak of China's tech-driven economic boom, DiDi emerged as China's leader in the world's largest, ride-hailing market, valued today at $64 billion globally.[11]

With deep pockets and powerful backers, DiDi surged ahead. A $2 billion funding round in 2015 was followed by another $4 billion in 2017 that helped the company to scale at a speed few could match. By 2018, DiDi was riding high, ranked as the second-most valuable startup in the world, trailing only the very company it had beaten on its own turf: Uber.[12]

It was a moment of national pride, China competing and winning in consumer tech. Building on this momentum, DiDi began expanding internationally in 2019, entering Latin America and other global markets. Its tactics of establishing strategic alliances, offering localized, innovative services, and emphasizing passenger safety demonstrated a remarkable ability to adapt and gain a significant market share, noted Evan A. Feigenbaum, Vice President for Studies, Carnegie Endowment for International Peace.[13]

Beijing vs. Wall Street

But beneath these triumphs, DiDi faced challenges in managing a sprawling, data-driven business in an era when Beijing's stance over big tech and data privacy was evolving. China's tech titans were being scrutinized for unfair and anticompetitive practices and handling of data.

Aggressively expanding, DiDi proceeded to go public in June 2021 on the NYSE despite signals from Chinese regulators to delay due to unresolved cybersecurity concerns. DiDi raised $4.4 billion in the largest US IPO of a Chinese company on a US exchange since Alibaba in 2014. But, just days after, the Chinese launched an investigation of its data practices and suspended DiDi from domestic app stores. Existing customers could continue using the service, but new user registrations were suspended. Ridership declined.

DiDi had misread the political climate in timing the IPO, and trust among investors was eroded. Under pressure from Beijing, DiDi announced in late 2021 it would delist from the NYSE. DiDi's market value plunged by about 85 percent from the IPO peak to the delisting process.

The turbulence didn't end there. In July 2022, the Chinese authorities fined DiDi $1.2 billion, citing data breaches related to cybersecurity and privacy concerns over cross-border data transfers.[14] Meanwhile, investors filed lawsuits alleging that DiDi concealed government directives to postpone its IPO until data privacy and security concerns were resolved.[15]

When DiDi's app was reinstated in app stores in January 2023, ridership quickly surged to nearly 29 million rides per day.[16] It was proof of some staying power despite increasing car ownership.[17]

In May 2024, DiDi co-founder Jean Liu, a former Goldman Sachs managing director and the daughter of Lenovo founder Liu Chuanzhi, resigned as president and board director. She transitioned into a new position as chief people officer, focusing on long-term strategy and corporate responsibility. This followed passenger safety issues that led to the company shutdown in 2018 of a social car-pooling service that had been promoted with features that allowed passengers and drivers to rate each other by appearance. Two female customers had allegedly been raped and murdered by drivers.

I had attended a DiDi event back in 2018, when Liu and the company's top executives laid out their vision with striking polish and confidence. The tone then was one of boundless ambition. Now, Liu and cofounder Cheng Wei, a former manager at Alibaba and Alipay, were humbly responding to the crisis, and publicly stated: "We will now prioritize safety as the most important performance indicator. We raced nonstop, riding on the force of breathless expansion and capital through these few years; but this has no meaning in such a tragic loss of life."

Remarkably, DiDi has remained the dominant ride-hailing service in China and held onto a market share of more than 70 percent. Tech titan Meituan has launched a rival service, and Alibaba-backed AutoNavi, too, has gotten into ride-hailing.

In this more restrained period of China's tech evolution, DiDi is no longer trumpeting new initiatives and is keeping a lower profile. The company had previously gone on an expansion spree internationally but is now less aggressive on that front and is focused more on the core Chinese market, the source of a vast majority of its revenues.

International Push a Must

In the go-go year of 2018, DiDi CEO Cheng Wei stated globalization as a "top strategic priority."[18] DiDi began offering an English-language interface and payment by international credit cards as well as WeChat pay and Alipay.

When the company expanded to 14 countries and worldwide, it counted 631 million annual users and 25 million drivers.[19] Even after the management crisis over safety issues, Didi regained momentum in its core ride-hailing business, and showed steady revenue gains, particularly in international, and was able to exit loss-making businesses.[20]

Not all geographic expansions worked out well, however—notably retreats from South Africa, Russia, Kazakhstan, and Taiwan plus the scuttling of European ambitions. Yet Latin America has been a success, except for a food delivery service the ride-hailing company tried. The region was ripe for convenient services because of urbanization, poor public transportation, and reduced availability of private cars.

In Brazil, DiDi took direct aim at Uber, investing $100 million in 2017 in Uber's key rival service, 99 Taxis, and acquiring it a year later at a $1 billion valuation. In Mexico, DiDi gained traction to nearly 60 percent of the ride-hailing market, bypassing Uber. DiDi won the competition against Uber due to a localized approach and understanding of the culture. The company catered to local preferences and needs such as offering credit cards, debit cards, loans, and insurance for drivers.[21]

In Asia and Australasia, DiDi has had mixed results. DiDi entered the Australian market in 2018, but lags established regional market leader Uber there. DiDi entered Japan in 2019 through a partnership with SoftBank but encountered stiff competition from local players and is limited to providing taxi-hailing services only through licensed partners. Likewise, in Hong Kong, restrictions meant Didi could offer only a taxi-booking service.

DiDi kept digging, investing for a stake in ride-hailing leaders Grab in Singapore and Ola in India. Japanese tech conglomerate SoftBank pursued the same opportunity, with a regional competitive service in each hotspot. Interestingly, in a repeat of Uber's saga in China—which DiDi won—Grab acquired Uber's Southeast Asian business in 2018, then merged the business into its own platform.

Diversification has been part of DiDi's gameplan, too—although not to the extent of other Chinese empire builders like Alibaba during the boom years. DiDi ventured into financial services accepting credit card applications and offering installment purchases, through a partnership with China Merchants Bank. DiDi also launched an autonomous trucking business with a fleet that shuttles between Tianjin and Inner Mongolia.

On the clean energy front, DiDi teamed up in 2019 with oil and gas multinational BP to build out an electric vehicle (EV) charging infrastructure in China, with the first units in Guangzhou. Additionally, DiDi co-launched a mass-market EV brand named NOMA, after selling its smart car development project to the Chinese EV maker. DiDi has delved further into autonomous driving technologies with other partnerships. With a $149 million investment in 2023 from two state-affiliated investors in Guangzhou, DiDi is working on commercializing and upgrading ride services in the southern province. DiDi also aims to get into robotaxis, supported by $298 million from Guangzhou Automobile Group and its EV subsidiary GAC Aion. DiDi is seeking substantially more funding for additional research and development to get its robotaxis on roads.

Surviving But Not So Great

Now, as the road ahead looks less bumpy for DiDi, there's speculation that the company could go public in Hong Kong. But no specific plans or a timeline have been confirmed.

DiDi's roller-coaster journey—from market dominance to regulatory crackdowns to financial struggles the beginnings of a rebound—stands out as an example of Chinese perseverance. But it also underscores the political risks for China's emerging companies. Once one of China's bold, ambitious power players, DiDi is a survivor but will need to continue to drill down on efficiencies and steady performance, before it can reclaim its status.

CHAPTER 8

CHINA'S DYNAMIC ONLINE SHOPS

Chinese e-commerce brands Temu and Shein have outpaced traditional e-retailers such as Alibaba and Amazon with snazzy merchandising, duty-free goods, and social commerce but face new challenges such as tariffs in their pursuit of US sales.

When China's shopping app Temu splashed two 30-second commercials during Super Bowl 2023, it sent shock waves through the industry. Who ever heard of Temu? Why was a Chinese brand on America's most-watched broadcast? How did an upstart from China afford the $7 million price tag for each ad?

But many millennials and Gen Z shoppers in the US were already quite familiar with Temu's online department store offering ultra-low prices. And now more Americans are too, because of US policies that have put China e-tailers at the center of the trade war.

Temu has sold low-priced yoga pants, gadgets, toys, kitchenware, and sneakers, fulfilling orders speedily through extensive supply chains, and shipping merchandise to US customer doorsteps within 10 days in individually addressed packages. China's Temu and online marketplace Shein have competed hard with retail giants Amazon and Walmart in the fast-paced e-commerce market. Within just a few years, Chinese e-commerce newcomers grabbed a significant share of US online retail sales.[1]

They gained customers through aggressive and creative sales tactics—social media influencers, group buying, livestreaming, AI-powered personalized shopping recommendations, flash sales, reward games, and unbeatable prices. E-tailer Shein has stood out for marketing the latest fashions with Facebook and Instagram posts from celebrities and everyday users who promote $5 colorful T-shirts and gorgeous $20 women's dresses—at a fraction of the cost of apparel retailers H&M and Zara.

Browsing on Temu and Shein is like being inside a digital arcade or casino rather than a shopping mall. It's fundamentally different from Amazon in that it encourages shoppers to buy now with a single click.[2] Temu surged to a $54 billion business based on Chinese merchants selling low-priced goods directly to the US, its largest market. Online fashions seller Shein skyrocketed to $38 billion,[3] with one-third of its revenues coming from the US. Known for super-fast uptake on trends, Shein tracks clothing trends, analyzes real-time data on sales, and produces the top-selling items quickly. Both brands smartly use AI extensively to forecast sales and adjust production and inventory for efficiency.

Temu and Shein could offer low prices partly because of a loophole known as the *de minimus* exemption that allowed goods worth less than $800 to be shipped to the US duty free. As many as 210 million packages were drop-shipped to US customers annually. As trade issues got into the spotlight in the new Trump administration, the White House closed this loophole. Tariffs were tacked on. The online Chinese sellers proceeded to hike prices, double or way more. Their sales dropped immediately. But don't count them out. Temu and Shein are finding workarounds that continue to keep their businesses humming. Chinese e-commerce contenders are agile and adept and will still be able to compete with US rivals Walmart and Amazon, said retail advisory analyst Deborah Weinswig, CEO and founder of Coresight Research.[4]

Weinswig appears to be right. Both have strategically adjusted logistics and sales strategies to try to maintain position but their products will cost more. Temu has stepped up expansion of US warehousing and distribution centers to fulfill orders[5] and also tacked on import charges for customers buying direct from China.[6] Shein has continued to ship merchandise directly from China to the US and has expanded its supply chain to include Vietnam for lower tariffs. The two disruptive innovators are also looking to expand into other large retail markets such as Brazil and Europe. Going overseas has been a priority for both companies, given the sluggish Chinese economy.

This tariff loophole change is welcomed by US retailers. They have argued that these Chinese entrants to the US had an unfair pricing advantage and were flooding the market with counterfeits and low-quality items. Concerns were also raised over the environmental impact of their mass production business. A congressional investigation highlighted unfair labor practices and human rights abuses, specifically in the Xinjiang region of China.[7] Calls for further scrutiny over other anticompetitive issues and legislative action were made by policy research groups. "Temu, in effect, is an information-gathering spyware program masquerading as an e-commerce site," wrote Diano Rinaldo, senior associate at the Center for Strategic and International Studies in Washington, DC.[8]

That sounds extreme. But the ongoing US–China trade and tech battles are definitely heated in fast-paced e-retailing.

A Necessary Wake-up Call

The popularity of these Chinese shopping apps should have been a wakeup call for American online retailers. Downloads of these apps were topping the US charts.[9] Shoppers on Temu were spending $247 annually and making six purchases each year, and 70 percent were repeat buyers.[10]

Established American retailers were slow to recognize and respond to this direct-from-China threat to their business. They didn't adjust their pricing strategies and supply chains as these bold movers from China outpaced them. US fashion retailer Forever 21 recently filed for bankruptcy and closed all 354 US stores.

Now Walmart and Amazon are fighting back by introducing competitive services. Amazon launched "Amazon Haul," a mobile app displaying fashion, beauty products, and electronics at "crazy-low prices" with delivery times matching Chinese rivals.[11] Meanwhile, Walmart relaunched its No Boundaries brand, going after Gen-Z with apparel and accessories priced mostly under $15.[12]

It hasn't been just Temu and Shein charging into Main Street USA. There are several made-in-China e-commerce contenders:

- **Temu**, the overseas subsidiary of China's Nasdaq-listed social commerce player Pinduoduo, launched in the US in 2022, runs its e-commerce app from Boston, and ships from China and warehouses in the US. Parent company PDD moved headquarters from Shanghai to Ireland in 2023.

- **Shein**, the fast fashion e-retailer focused on global markets, started in Nanjing in 2008 as a wedding dress seller, pivoted to fashions by the early 2010s, and moved operations to Singapore in 2022, selling directly to the US, Europe, and Japan from "Shein village" factory hubs in Guangzhou. An IPO in London was eyed, but trade tensions and a stalled approval from China led to a recent switch to Hong Kong.
- **Xiaohongshu**, or RedNote in the West, the Chinese startup that blends e-commerce and social media, and became high profile as an alternative to a possible TikTok ban in the US.
- **Douyin**, or **TikTok** outside China, the ByteDance-owned short video app that has popularized livestreaming e-commerce.
- **Kuaishou**, the short video and livestreaming app that moved into e-commerce and went public in Hong Kong in 2021.
- **AliExpress**, the global online marketplace launched by Alibaba in 2010, offering gadgets and niche items, mostly shipped directly from China independent sellers at wholesale-style prices, but losing ground to newer platform Temu.

China Takes to E-Commerce in a Big Way

E-commerce was a new concept in the digital arena in the 1980s and took off with the launch of Amazon in 1995 in the US and Alibaba in 1999 in China. Online buying and selling grew to one-fifth of retail sales globally. Quick to adopt new digital trends, China became the world's largest e-commerce market, reaching an estimated $3.6 trillion, or almost half of global transactions,[13] way ahead of the US at $1.2 trillion.[14] Almost two-thirds of China's 1.4 billion citizens and 88 percent of internet users shop online,[15] meaning just about everyone. For comparison, about three-quarters of the US population have shopped for items online.[16]

Jack Ma Started It

China's e-commerce revolution traces back to 1999 when Jack Ma formed Alibaba to power up small and medium-sized businesses on the internet. China's most famous entrepreneur supersized his startup into dominance. He famously trounced eBay with the launch of consumer marketplace Taobao in 2003 for individual sellers. Then he added Tmall in 2011 for global brands and retailers. He expanded to digital payments in 2004 with Alipay, a platform that evolved into Ant Financial, later rebranded as Ant Group. Alibaba capitalized on China's mobile-first internet society—and then beat Amazon in China with aggressive pricing, promotion, and features that appealed to locals.

Alibaba's fiercest rival, JD.com, jumped into the e-commerce business in 2004. JD.com has prioritized rapid, efficient shipments from an extensive logistics network. Walmart invested in JD.com in 2016 to gain a large foothold in China and collaborate on fulfillment and delivery. But when sales slowed at JD.com in an increasingly competitive market, the US retail giant sold its near 10 percent stake in 2024 for $3.6 billion and turned to expanding its own operations in China, mainly through Sam's Club warehouse stores. More recently, JD.com has refocused on a core business of supply chain operations.

In China's giant local e-commerce market today, innovation has meant leadership. Nimble upstarts with social commerce have gained fast. The biggest disruptor is Pinduoduo, the parent company of Temu, which surpassed JD.com and captured one-quarter of China online sales.[17] PDD Holdings has chipped away at Alibaba's lead, which has shrunk to 42 percent,[18] and has surpassed the tech titan in market capitalization. At the same time, Douyin—the Chinese version of TikTok—is surging ahead into commerce, signaling that the disruption is far from over.

"Alibaba and JD got complacent and were resting on their laurels."

—Michael Zakkour,
founder of digital consulting firm
5 New Digital

"Alibaba and JD got complacent and were resting on their laurels," said Michael Zakkour, founder of digital consulting firm 5 New Digital. "Newcomers were able to grab market share from Alibaba and JD. They did a better job of reading the consumer in China. They prioritized value, speed, personalization, and gamification beyond simply presenting another marketplace that acts like another catalog."

Chinese contender Pinduoduo came up with the concept of making online shopping a social experience. Its business model shifted from traditional search-based shopping to interactive, community-driven social commerce. "PDD invented the first true social commerce platform. It showed the world that you can build social personal first and then grow a business from there," said digital consultant Zakkour. China has been ahead of the rest of the world in adopting these new retail technologies to shopping, he pointed out.

Social Shopping Madness

PDD's imaginative billionaire founder Colin Huang has described his original business as similar to discount retailer Costco mixed with entertainment property Disneyland. Loosely translated as "much more together," Pinduoduo is like a giant flea market on mobile, with built-in games and social networking and discounts and coupons for restaurants, travel, and attractions.

On the app, bargain hunters select an item to purchase, and then invite friends, family, and social connections to click and buy online with them. Consumers can team up to share bulk discounts, play games with lucky draws, and click on flash sales to drive impulse purchases. AI-driven algorithms spin shopping recommendations to potential buyers.

Original investor James Mi, founding partner of VC firm Lightspeed China Partners, pointed out his portfolio company's disruptive business model. "Everybody thinks that China's BAT (Baidu, Alibaba, and Tencent) are so big that it would be impossible to disrupt them, but there's always a company in the garage that is going to come out and do something different," Mi told me soon after funding the startup in 2015, which went public on Nasdaq in 2018 and raised $1.6 billion. But founder Huang (at one time the richest man in China due to PDD's stock price) resigned in 2021 to focus on philanthropy as his company faced regulatory headwinds in China's big tech crackdown, and was slammed for quality, trust, and safety issues. Recouping, PDD prioritized improvements and updates, geared toward supporting high-quality merchants. At 10 years old, Pinduduo continues to chalk up strong revenue growth, a 33 percent increase in 2024 to $54 billion—although sales are slowing for subsidiary Temu in the US.

The Ascent of Little Red Book

In another corner is China's e-commerce player Xiaohongshu, or "Little Red Book" (no connection to Chairman Mao's quotations book). The Chinese-made brand carved out a niche by merging user-generated content with shopping experiences. Founded by Miranda Qu (who spoke at my Silicon Dragon Shanghai event in 2017) and Charlwin Mao in 2013, Xiaohongshu has a following of 312 million young, urban consumers who turn to the shopping platform for global beauty, fashion, and travel brands. The Instagram-like app is highly popular for product reviews written by regular customers and influencers. Typical posts are step-by-step guides on makeup, before-and-after makeover images, and photos of trying on clothes in a fitting room.

The success of RedNote, its Westernized nickname, has prompted legacy e-commerce platforms to follow the lead and integrate more social-driven content strategies to maintain user engagement. Interestingly, RedNote got a recent boost from a strategic tie-up with Alibaba that lets users directly click on links to shop online at Taobao. The partnership signaled the competitiveness of the market and the interactivity that's driving it.

RedNote capitalizes on the social aspect of shopping in China. Consumers rely on recommendations and reviews from peers often in video and livestreaming, select items, then search for in-depth reviews from key opinion leaders to confirm choices, before placing an order. Payment is processed through WeChat or Alipay. A key reason for the appeal of RedNote is the authentic reviews posted by other community members. Highly popular among millennial and Gen Z female urban residents, the app is a hotspot for beauty and fashion brands.

While not doing much outreach to the US, RedNote got a sudden boost as an alternative to TikTok during the recent noise about a potential ban of the video-sharing app in the US. In early 2025, when a TikTok shutdown seemed imminent, RedNote picked up more than 700,000 new users in just two days,[19] soon climbing to 300 million. A popular setting was switching the app from Mandarin to English.

The well-funded social shopping app has raised more than $900 million from investors including Tencent, Alibaba, Temasek, Sequoia China, and Hillhouse Capital. Its most recent valuation stands at $20 billion. This strong backing in addition to RedNote's fast growth of 30 percent annually to $4.8 billion revenues in 2024 have fueled speculation of an IPO on the horizon.[20]

Alligator in the River

The big contender in China online commerce has been aging but is seeking to regain its youthful spirit. From a startup in Hangzhou in 1999, Alibaba transformed into a global e-commerce and technology powerhouse. Founded by Jack Ma and 18 partners, the company focused on creating an online marketplace to connect Chinese manufacturers with overseas buyers. Over the past 25 years, the tech titan expanded its reach across cloud computing, AI, logistics, and fintech.

Alibaba's charismatic leader, Ma, was a great promoter of the company's mission to help small businesses in China enter the internet age. He helped to popularize the nation's Singles' Day (November 11 or Double 11) shopping festival of 24 hours with special pricing and promotions. With his characteristic soundbites, he proclaimed that, while Amazon is the shark in the ocean, Alibaba is the alligator in the river. He made headlines, too, when he visited Donald Trump in his first term, promising to create US jobs by helping small businesses sell to China on Alibaba's e-commerce sites. He rubbed shoulders with who's who at the World Economic Forum in Davos. Ma became an internet celebrity worldwide and a superhero in China.

Under Ma's leadership, Alibaba's influence continued to grow, leading to its record-breaking initial public offering on the New York Stock Exchange in 2014, raising $25 billion. His company diversified into several businesses related to e-commerce. Alibaba got into cloud computing with the 2009 launch of Alibaba Cloud, which in six years became China's largest cloud computing service, offering data processing and storage solutions. Alibaba jumped into the logistics business in 2013 by cofounding supply chain and warehousing startup Cainiao Network to improve delivery efficiency across China. Finally, he and his team built Alibaba overseas with AliExpress and investments in overseas entities such as regional e-commerce leader Lazada in Southeast Asia.

Sprawling Empire

By 2020, Alibaba's sprawling conglomerate reached annual revenues of $71.9 billion. But Alibaba's size, power, and influence over large sectors of the economy was squashed by the Chinese government's crackdown on tech titans' size and influence. After founder Ma criticized China's financial system as outdated and restrictive, he was summoned to a meeting and interview with Chinese regulators, who raised concerns that Alibaba's fintech's operations posed systemic financial risks. They ordered its fintech business, Ant Group, to operate more like a traditional bank, subject to stricter regulations and capital requirements.[21] A planned IPO of Ant was halted in 2020, which sent Alibaba's shares downward.[22]

Alibaba retrenched, pivoting back to its e-commerce roots. Assets were sold outside the core commerce and logistics businesses, and unprofitable businesses were shed to free up more resources to fend off aggressive newcomers. The Chinese e-commerce leader ditched stakes in China-based brick-and-mortar businesses including large hypermarket operator Sun Art Retail in early 2025 and department store chain Intime Retail Group a few months earlier. Alibaba also reduced holdings in China's electric vehicle maker Xpeng.

Alibaba withdrew from some international investments, too, although it maintains e-commerce business Lazada in the highly competitive Southeast Asia market. In India, Alibaba gradually exited investments in payments platform Paytm, food delivery business Zomato, and online grocery store BigBasket.

In a management shakeup in 2023 to reboot the company after a decentralization, co-founder and Ma's right-hand man Joe Tsai became chairman while cofounder Eddie Wu, the startup's first technology director who was instrumental in building out its mobile and payments businesses, was promoted to CEO. They put together the latest plank in a recovery plan: $53 billion of investment in cloud computing and AI over the next three years, exceeding the amount spent on these two technologies over the past decade. CEO Wu has likened AI to "the electricity of the future" and cloud computing to the "electricity grid," underscoring the foundational infrastructure and distribution channels (see Chapter 6).[23]

Alibaba Door Opener

In signs of a modest rebound, revenue growth at Alibaba has been picking up but not near the prior levels of 2020 and 2021 before regulatory scrutiny and a cooling domestic economy took its toll. Alibaba's launch of this new AI initiative has been well received, with shares trading up 14 percent soon after the strategy was announced. While improving, market capitalization is far from its pre-crackdown peak.

The most impactful sign of a rebound was when Ma joined a select group of the biggest names in Chinese technology and business at a summit convened in early 2025 by Chinese President Xi Jinping to encourage entrepreneurship and innovation. This meeting was seen as a door opener between China's entrepreneurial innovators and its government controllers, and an aid for its e-commerce titans to thrive in China—and elsewhere.

The success of Chinese e-commerce leaders globally has been an ability to innovate with new AI and social commerce technologies—sometimes ahead of the West. But as a new era for e-commerce is arriving, the market's fast pace and hyper-competitiveness coupled with uncertain trade battles and tariffs means that no one leader—newcomers or incumbents—can be assured of their staying power.

CHAPTER 9

CHINESE ELECTRIC VEHICLE MAKERS SPEED PAST

China has accelerated into the electric vehicle (EV) market with few U-turns, led by strong contenders BYD and Xiaomi, with innovation and pricing that threaten to leave Tesla behind. The next battle will be over autonomous driving. Plus, a Q&A with autotech expert Michael Dunne who sounds the alarm for Detroit.

Over the past quarter century of traveling to China, I've seen the nation undergo a remarkable transformation—from roads dominated by bicycles, carts, mopeds, and crowded buses to smart, connected EVs built by ambitious startups. Thanks to turbocharging government subsidies, China has accelerated into a nation on the move.

Tesla entered China in 2013 when EVs were new and different. I well recall Tesla's Shanghai-based executive Dan Hsu keynoting my Silicon Dragon forum in Shanghai and talking up how the American EV maker would bring its US playbook to China. A Tesla model was on display, and the futuristic sleek design drew a steady crowd of curious, admiring onlookers.[1]

Elon Musk went after the Chinese market aggressively, helped by substantial government support such as land grants, tax breaks, and subsidies. In 2019, Tesla built and opened the first fully foreign-owned auto plant in China, a gigafactory in Shanghai that allowed it to avoid import tariffs, cut costs, and speed up delivery times to Chinese consumers. Then, Tesla opened a new mega-factory in 2025 to manufacture energy storage batteries.

Tesla has marketed its Model 3 and Model Y to tech-savvy urban buyers, priced in the premium range starting $32,000. Those cars commanded 15 percent of China EV sales in the peak year 2020, but that's fallen significantly. The reason? Exploding sales from Chinese rivals with aggressive pricing, showy digital features, and strong local support. Beyond that, Tesla has lost its novelty appeal. Rising political tensions also have dampened its appeal, with consumers starting to prefer local brands. Tesla's main Chinese rival, Shenzhen-based BYD, has taken the market lead, selling an entry-level vehicle at below $10,000 and an extensive range of models in its lineup.[2] It was a decisive shift.

Tesla squeezed in China

China is Tesla's most critical battleground for the future, the American brand's second-largest market, after its home country. In 2024, Tesla faced its first sales decline worldwide (although the Model Y held on to the lead as the world's best-selling battery EV). China was the only major region where Tesla gained sales—up 8.8 percent,[3] albeit pumped by discounts.

Encountering strong competition in China, in early 2025 Tesla came out swinging, though with models that began to seem outdated next to the new Chinese EVs. It created a sales buzz by refreshing the Model Y with upgrades to the exterior design, cabin, and driving range. Then, later that year, Tesla introduced a family-sized, six-seater model that caters to China's preference for roomier interiors.

China is increasingly shaping the future of EVs. "The Chinese EV makers are advanced and are innovating at the cutting edge, and Tesla needs to be able to keep up with that," said tech expert and China adviser Paul Triolo. "China has the advantage because they have the supply chain for EVs, particularly rare earth minerals and batteries—and a big advantage in costs."

Dozens of Chinese EV brands, including such leaders as BYD, Xiaomi, NIO, Xpeng, and Zeekr, compete with Tesla. The market has become overcrowded, and many Chinese EV makers are unprofitable, partly due to heavy price discounting. Their flashy designs and feature-packed, interior infotainment screens with high-quality graphics are winning over customers. BYD gets points for its vertically integrated system of design and manufacturing, NIO for swappable batteries, Zeekr for its movable and adjustable seats that can swivel 270 degrees, and Xiaomi for its cool-looking, sporty cars and leverage of smartphone technology—just as some examples.

Raising the ante, Xiaomi (originally a smartphone maker), launched the YU7 sport utility vehicle in 2025 to add to its sedan the year before. The new SUV was touted as a Tesla killer and is slightly less expensive than the popular Model Y, which then cost around $36,600.

Checking out the competition, Ford CEO Jim Farley test drove the Xiaomi sedan, which his company flew from Shanghai. After six months of driving it, Farley admitted he didn't want to give it up.[4]

Leading the World in EVs

Seemingly overnight, China has become a world leader in making and selling EVs. About 70 percent of EVs globally are manufactured in China, and Chinese EVs claim about two-thirds of total EVs sold worldwide. And get this: about half of passenger cars purchased in China are electric or plug-in hybrids, and that's projected to reach 60 percent within a year, boosted by government subsidies, lower prices, availability of EV charging stations—not to mention a vast auto supply chain network. Compare this to the US: electric car sales are growing by 10 percent but still only account for one in 10 vehicles sold nationwide. The outlook for EV sales in the US is unclear given less governmental support such as phasing out of tax credits for new EV buyers.[5]

Across China's cities, EV charging stations are springing up (well more than 10 million in 2025) and could soon outnumber gas stations, as they do in Shenzhen already.[6] With battery charging taking about the same time as pumping gas and providing a driving range of up to 400 miles for some models, this future is arriving fast, and China is ahead.

"I hate to say I told you so. For several years I've been talking with policymakers that the only way the US automakers will compete globally with Chinese firms is by adopting standard battery swapping technology or open standard rapid charging. We are woefully behind," commented venture capitalist Gary Rieschel, referring to China's strides in developing five-minute EV charging times, led by BYD and battery maker CATL. "The Chinese EVs are going to absolutely dominate the world. It's not even going to be close," he said in an interview with me.

At the center of this Chinese automotive revolution is China's "Gang of Five"—leading EV innovators with futuristic technologies. The car of tomorrow can drive and park without a human hand on the steering wheel. The interior is a living room on wheels, designed for comfort with built-in food trays, footrests, pillows, and interactive mobile screens—features that make business-class airline travel look skimpy.

The Xiaomi-made smart car is so popular that Chinese customers line up to tour the company's highly automated EV factory in Beijing. Tickets are distributed by lottery, and free slots resell for up to $280, noted China tech observer Rui Ma. The tour includes a technology exhibition, a walkthrough of the production line, and a test drive. One assembly line produces 20,000 vehicles per month with approximately 100 human workers. The rest of the work is done by robotic arms and automated systems. But as she pointed out, "What feels cutting-edge today may seem outdated within just a few years."[7]

The Warren Buffett-backed BYD, the world's leading EV seller, is earning high praise for luxury brand Yangwang, which comes equipped with a God's Eye intelligent navigation system. With advanced technologies, the newest model can drive on three wheels, lift up to dodge obstacles, do a 360-degree turn, slide sideways into tight parking spots, and, in an emergency mode, can float and drive on water for up to 30 minutes.[8]

But try to buy one in the US! These vehicles aren't produced or sold in America. High tariffs on Chinese goods, a lack of dealer networks, and national security concerns have blocked the Chinese EVs from entering.

The idea of China's new EVs on US highways has triggered competitive concerns and data security alarms on Capitol Hill about data collection and transmission from foreign (read China)-made vehicles. "Ideally, the green tech auto sector would be kept out of the US–China tech competition. But

US automakers would not like the competition, even though they're not producing $15,000 or $20,000 EVs," said Triolo, in an interview with me. "There will be an anti-China fervor if Chinese automakers are allowed to build facilities in the US. This would have to include moving the manufacture of Chinese batteries too."

Triolo suggested that a possible—though difficult—solution is to allow Chinese EV makers to invest in the US, provided that data collected from connected cars is protected and stored locally, within the US.

Techie-first automakers

Unlike the old guard of Detroit, the founders of China's leading EV companies are technologists first, not traditional carmakers. They rely on technical knowhow plus access to capital, connections, government support—and a global vision. A few were tech billionaires first before becoming automakers. For instance, He Xiaopeng (b. 1977) founded Guangzhou-based EV innovator Xpeng Motors in 2018 after making a fortune from Alibaba's acquisition of his mobile browser startup for a record-breaking $4 billion in 2014. I interviewed him in Mountain View, California, at the company's R&D facility for autonomous driving, soon after the 2018 release of a sporty-looking, compact SUV in China. His career mirrored the techie path of Elon Musk, who leapt from digital startup PayPal to Tesla. The Xpeng founder told me, through a translator, that his "goal was to make a global intelligent mobility company." The next, new thing for Xpeng could be flying cars, which have been in concept stage and are planned for liftoff in late 2026. This so-called eVTOL, or electric vehicle takeoff and landing vehicle, detaches from a six-wheeled Xpeng van and then takes off, drawing power from the van's batteries and controlled by mobile app. On display at the Consumer Electronics Show in 2025, it drew a lot of gawkers, but sadly no demos.

Since the early 1980s, China has wanted to develop its own powerful auto industry. Now China has realized that goal through its leading technology companies, observed automotive consultant Michael Dunne. China's homegrown tech-oriented startups are powering up in the electric and self-driving market, and are referred to as the Gang of Five (see Table 9.1). Dunne was certainly prescient in his prediction six years ago that China "could make world-class vehicles with their smart and cashed-up tech companies. By relying on tech companies instead of the entrenched automakers, they have found their point of leverage. They can make a great leap forward with scale, regulations, technology, and a capital river of billions. I think the US is in trouble."[9] See my full interview with Dunne at the end of this chapter.

Advanced Driving Or Not?

The next battle coming is over autonomous driving technology. There are two different standards—China and US.

Tesla's "full self-driving" system has faced regulatory and tech hurdles in China, which led to a rebranding of its FSD feature as intelligent assistant driving in China to better reflect the reality that the cars don't fully drive themselves.[10] Tesla started rolling out a limited version of the FSD system in China, priced at $8,800, and has been aiming toward a full launch but has run into other hurdles.[11] Tesla's autopilot system relies on a network of tiny exterior cameras and software updates. But

Table 9.1

China's "Gang of Five" EV makers

BYD (Build Your Dreams)

- Based in Shenzhen, BYD is China's largest EV maker and is a global leader in battery technology
- Transitioned from battery manufacturer to autos to EVs
- Strong backing from Warren Buffett's Berkshire Hathaway
- Produces a wide range of EVs, including pure electric and plug-in hybrid models
- Expanding aggressively into international markets, including Europe, Southeast Asia, and Latin America
- Founded by battery engineer and chemist Wang Chuanfu in 1994
- Listed on the Hong Kong Stock Exchange in 2002 and on the Shanghai Stock Exchange in 2011

NIO

- Located in Shanghai, known for its premium electric SUVs and sedans
- Founded in 2014
- Pioneered battery-swapping technology, allowing drivers to replace depleted batteries within minutes
- Once touted as the Tesla of China
- Focuses on high-end EVs with advanced features such as AI-powered infotainment and autonomous driving
- Expanding in Europe, starting with Norway, Germany, and other key markets
- Founded by tech billionaire William Li in who took online car sales platform BitAuto public on the New York Stock Exchange
- Went public on the New York Stock Exchange in 2018
- Significant government investment from the city of Hefei after nearly going bankrupt in 2020

Xpeng (Xiaopeng Motors)

- A tech-driven EV startup headquartered in Guangzhou with smart features and its own autonomous driving system, XNGP
- Competes directly with Tesla in China, offering advanced driver-assistance systems
- Expanding into Europe and other overseas markets
- Tech billionaire founder He Xiaopeng sold prior startup UCWeb to Alibaba for $4.3 billion in 2014
- Founded Xpeng in 2014
- IPO on the New York Stock Exchange in 2020

Li Auto

- Specializes in extended-range electric vehicles (EREVs), which use a small gasoline engine for longer journeys
- Based in Beijing and focuses on large, family-oriented SUVs with high efficiency
- Rapidly growing sales and expanding its model lineup
- Founded in 2015 by Li Xiang, who previously formed an online car information and sales platform
- Listed on Nasdaq in 2020

Geely (Zhejiang Geely Holding Group)

- Large traditional automaker owns Volvo, Polestar, and Lotus, and has an investment stake in Daimler (Mercedes-Benz)
- Produces a mix of electric and hybrid vehicles under brands such as premium EVs Zeekr and Geometry
- Headquartered in Hangzhou and expanding globally through strategic partnerships and acquisitions
- Billionaire industrialist and auto tycoon Li Shufu founded auto division of Geely in 1997 and Zeekr in 2021
- Listed on the Hong Kong Stock Exchange since 2005; its subsidiary Zeekr went public on the New York Stock Exchange in 2024

Chinese approvals for software updates and strict data privacy laws have presented roadblocks. Tesla has been prevented from using locally gathered driving data in China to train its autonomous driving algorithms like it does in the US.[12]

Additionally, tests of Tesla's advanced driving software got off to a rocky start. One test driver in China likened the experience to a foreigner getting lost in China driving on unknown roads.[13] There were incorrect lane changes and misleading traffic signals, due to a lack of local data training. The fix? Tesla started collaborating in 2025 with Chinese tech giant Baidu to integrate navigation and detailed mapping data and localize the self-driving features for roads in China.

Unlike Tesla with built-in cameras and AI systems for navigation, the Chinese makers rely on laser and LIDAR sensors for self-driving technology. Xiaomi, Xpeng, BYD, and others have launched their own advanced driver assistance systems, increasingly offered as a standard feature on most models. BYD EV buyers recently got a free tech upgrade to its advanced God's Eye navigational system.

The vehicle maker that can deliver on the promise of autonomous driving in China will win, tech consultant Triolo told me. "To compete in China, Tesla is going to have to have their full self-driving capability in China trained on China road data." But US–China geopolitics may get in the way. As Triolo points out, "Now Tesla can't import the advanced GPUs (used in AI and machine learning) to train the full self-driving system. They're going to run into a problem if their self-driving is not as good as Chinese cars."

Tesla is up against the so-called "Gang of Five" EV makers outlined in Table 9.1. There is also a sixth—China's tech giant Huawei fits into this group of EV makers as a provider of intelligent driving systems.

Robotaxis on the Way

The next phase of China's transportation revolution is robotaxis, or AI-driven passenger shuttles. As with other technologies, China studies US leaders first, then is quick to commercialize products. Of particular interest has been Google and tests of its Waymo self-driving vehicles, which began in 2019 and are now fairly commonplace in San Francisco and Phoenix. Now China is pulling ahead of the West in testing driverless vehicles on roads. Autopilot tests are going on in

16 Chinese cities, and 19 Chinese companies and their suppliers are competing for position.[14] The US remains off limits to the China contenders due to national security concerns over Chinese-made software in connected cars and robotaxis. Meanwhile, Tesla has launched its own robotaxi projects in a limited way in Austin with plans to expand to other cities and is preparing to produce a "Cybercab" with no steering wheel or pedals in 2026.[15]

In China, tech titan Baidu is in the forefront of launching driverless cars through its Apollo Go. These robotaxis have taken more 11 million passengers for a ride in several Chinese megacities since 2021, and Baidu has begun charging for the service. Trials were recently started near Hong Kong International Airport, and in Abu Dhabi and Dubai through partnerships. Contrast Baidu's progress with General Motors' failure, pulling the plug on money-losing Cruise robotaxi service in 2024 after a decade of development.

Two other Chinese players in this emerging space are WeRide and Toyota-backed Pony AI, which focus on China but have made forays into the Middle East, Europe, and South Korea. Backed by major automakers and chip makers, and leading venture capitalists, WeRide (supported by Nvidia and Nissan) and Pony AI (backed by Toyota) went public on Nasdaq in late 2024.

But getting to commercialization or profitability has been another matter. Most of the driverless rides are offered for free. Limited tests of paid rides in specific routes in China, such as to and from the newish Beijing Daxing International Airport, have been ongoing but profitability is still distant. Yet robotaxis are catching on in limited zones and tech-savvy spots in China—ahead of the US.

Slow regulations, safety concerns, and less government support of alternatives to the treasured private car in the US have limited the appeal of driverless robotic shuttles—and electric vehicles, too. The future of transportation could be another area where America may have to face being second.

How China is Winning the Electric Vehicle Race

Revealing Q&A with China autotech expert Michael Dunne

Originally from Detroit, Michael Dunne went to China right out of school from the University of Michigan. He spent 26 years in Asia, where he was president of GM Indonesia, founded a car internet portal, led J.D. Power's research business in China, and then set up advisory firm Dunne Insights in San Diego to advise companies on future trends in China, electrics, autonomous vehicles, and mobility.

Dunne recalls attending a summit in Beijing where China began its push to dominate the EV market. The minister of science and technology, Wang Gang, started it off by saying, "Great news. China has now surpassed the US. We're the number-one producer of cars in the world. We're the number-one buyer of cars in the world. I should be a happy man, but I'm not. Why am I not happy? Number one, we're now the biggest oil importer in the world. Two, the skies are terrible. And three, I don't see any Chinese cars on the road. They're all foreign cars. So what are we going to do about this? We need to change dramatically. Let's go electric." Dunne recalls that, when the government official said that in 2009, everybody in the audience thought, "That's a crazy idea. That's not going to happen." But soon, China went down that road with a well-marked map.

Sounding the Alarm for Detroit

Today, China produces one-third of the world's passenger vehicles, and its share could climb to 40 percent while GM and Ford are losing ground and a Stellantis joint venture to make Jeeps in China failed. China's gains are largely driven by EVs. Almost half of cars sold in China are electric, up from 6 percent in 2022—compared with 10 percent in the US. Moreover, China builds more EVs than all other countries combined—12.4 million in 2024.

In this interview with the author, Michael Dunne outlines how China is shaking up the global automotive underscore market with top-selling new EVs. The italics highlight key messages.

Fannin: **How powerful is China becoming in the automotive market worldwide?**

Dunne: The ground that was so solid for global automakers for so long in China has just vanished. It's like an earthquake. China is 50 percent bigger than the next biggest market. China now has the capacity to supply half the world's demand for cars. We've never seen anything like this, not Japan and Korea at their peaks.

Fannin: **Is China's gain mostly related to electric vehicles?**

Dunne: Yes, inside China, there's this sudden rush to electrics. But of the 6 million exports China will do this year, 75 percent are gasoline-powered vehicles. What's going on there? Most of those exports are going to developing countries where people are less interested in buying electric. Most are coming from Chinese plants, for example, SOEs such as Chery that were building gasoline-powered vehicles that the market in China no longer wants. They've got this idle capacity, so they're shipping it.

Fannin: **What can the US carmakers do to catch up or speed ahead?**

Dunne: It always comes down to innovation. The onc company that's holding its own against the Chinese and doing admirably so globally is, of course, Tesla. And what separates Tesla from everyone else is they're constantly innovating—with batteries, with autonomous vehicle technologies, and software. The key differentiator for cars in the future will be who does software best. That means, when you get in your car and hit the navigation button to figure out where you want to go, that's really easy, simple and quick. You want entertainment, you hit some buttons. No hitches. The Chinese have gotten very good at this. Tesla's very good at this. Everybody's racing to get better at software.

Volkswagen invested in XPeng, founded by one of the Chinese tech titans. That's a very interesting play. What VW sees in Xpeng is an opportunity to learn what's the cutting edge in software and autonomy. Stellantis has bought a stake in a Chinese company called Leapmotor for access to its strengths in batteries and electric vehicles, but also software. *The idea is if we can't beat them, let's buy into them and figure out what the hell they're doing.*

Fannin: **Have Ford or GM followed the VW and Stellantis tech investment model for their China operations?**

Dunne: They have not done so. It's a little bit of a puzzle. GM was one of several investors in an autonomous technology company called Momenta, but no, that's not a game changer. And Ford, no, they've been looking, but they haven't pulled the trigger on any kind of investment like we've seen with Stellantis and VW.

Fannin: **Are the Chinese copycatting or innovating?**

Dunne: Oh, they're definitely innovating, but in ways that borrow heavily from knowledge that they've secured from the West. For many years, China's leading autonomous vehicle companies such as Baidu, Pony AI, and others were camped in California and hiring. This was starting in 2015–16, hiring the best and brightest from wherever they could come – Google or Apple or Tesla. At a peak, there were 14 companies testing autonomous vehicles on California roads. For various political reasons, most of them have decamped back to China, but imagine all those years of acquired knowledge.

Fannin: **What happened to those Chinese R&D facilities in California?**

Dunne: Those have shrunk down. There's been increased vigilance by the US government. 'What's your business here? What are you doing with the technology? Why? What's your purpose?' *One by one, we've seen the Chinese EV makers return to China and say, we'll take our gathered knowledge, build on it with incremental improvements, and deploy in China.*

Fannin: **What are China's manufacturing strengths with self-driving technology?**

Dunne: China is a beast of a manufacturing machine, the likes of which we have not seen before, the scale, the technology, the subsidies, the supply chains are, at least for now, unmatched. In China, it's "How do we move this along more quickly? We understand it's going to be a major differentiator for us as a nation to be first in autonomy. So let's get this thing going."

***Fannin:* What's your view of the quality of Chinese EV makers?**

Dunne: Some of the Chinese companies are very impressive, but not all are cut out of the same thread. Some are really legitimate, world-class automakers, and BYD being the best example. BYD is the Toyota of China, a class by its own—the market leader. Globally, BYD is on track to surpass Ford, and it's the number one maker of EVs. BYD has its own batteries and supply chains. They're vertically integrated, they're low cost. *BYD is a force, and that keeps other automakers around the world up at night. They're taking share everywhere they go.*

***Fannin:* Why has Warren Buffett been selling his shares in BYD?**

Dunne: You have to imagine that geopolitics is part of the reason why.

***Fannin:* Are Chinese electric carmakers a good bet for investors?**

Dunne: There's massive overcapacity in their home market. With so many players, a price war is driving margins down to zero or below. Many Chinese automakers in the EV space are losing money today. Only BYD and a startup Li Auto are making money. Most others are either breaking even or losing in the EV space. Maybe XPeng, which is invested in by VW, might pull things together and start making money. But for now, it's a risky bet. It's not clear who the winners will be and where the profits will come from.

***Fannin:* Nio was promoted a few years ago as the Tesla of China. How's Nio doing?**

Dunne: Nio is going to be a spectacular success, or drown in just too many costs. Their strategy is to build out thousands of places to swap batteries. Those are expensive to build and maintain. William Li, the founder, is saying it's a differentiator. Up until now, it's been hit and miss.

***Fannin:* What other Chinese automakers have promising business models?**

Dunne: The most exciting company in the last year or two has been the emergence of Xiaomi into the auto space. Xiaomi is doing essentially what Apple set out to do when it launched Project Titan, back in 2014—and that is to build a computer on wheels. Xiaomi took all their knowledge of smartphones and building, and launched their first car in 2024. It's called the SU7, and it's met with spectacular demand inside China. It looks like a cross between a Porsche and a Tesla, and it features all of the most up-to-date software that you'd find on your smartphone.

***Fannin:* Can these China's tech companies make it in the auto market, too?**

Dunne: The founders made their money in software. What's the next, next new thing? Cars. You have Xpeng, Lee Auto, Nio, and Xiaomi. *I call these companies the Gang of Five—all run by software billionaires.*

***Fannin:* How does Huawei compete in this market?**

Dunne: Huawei is in the market in a creative and interesting way. Huawei is bringing the features of software, autonomous driving, and infotainment to SOEs in China that were sitting on a lot of overcapacity in joint ventures building gasoline vehicle engines. Huawei has gone to EV makers and said, you build a car, and we'll bring the brains for these features. So far, it looks like it's working.

***Fannin:* Of the Gang of Five, who's going to win in the Chinese EV market?**

Dunne: You've got BYD as an established, legit, global player already. Then you have Geely, which has invested in or acquired Volvo, Lotus Cars, Polestar, and EV brand Zeekr. They're going to be a force in this business, too. They have EVs, they have gasoline, they have hybrids. They're so large and international, they're flexible, and they have a billionaire founder. The issue is always, let's not get big company disease. Let's keep driving.

I think you have to give Xiaomi the best odds of making it. They have established businesses with a lot of cash flow from other areas. And Xiaomi has an advantage in placing cars in distribution points around the country where they sell phones.

***Fannin:* How do US consumers regard the Chinese autos?**

Dunne: The first take is, just a big thought bubble with a giant question mark—"Like Chinese carmakers, what?" If I asked 100 people on the street in San Diego to name China's top three automakers, 99 would fail. They are curious about Chinese carmakers, as an interesting concept. They might ask, what are their names? Or they may have heard that Chinese are really good at electrics, and want to know where they can get their hands on some affordable vehicles from China.

***Fannin:* How is Tesla doing in China, considering increased competition from Chinese EVs?**

Dunne: Tesla had first mover advantage when they got going in 2020 with their mega-factory in Shanghai. They were clearly the market leader, no question about it, and they continue to do well there. Half of Tesla's global production is in China. Tesla is supplying the Chinese market and exporting to dozens of other countries around the world. Elon's not comfortable unless he's living right on the edge. And he's living right on the edge with China. Initially, he was competing against established players like SOEs and gasoline carmakers converting to electric. Now he's surrounded. From below, he has BYD, which is super cost effective, and sells cars that cost $20,000. Then left and right, he has formidable competitors, Xiaomi and Huawei and XPeng and Li Auto saying, "Yeah, we like your business, and we like the premiums you make." So their cars are priced at or above Tesla. *If you look at the top 12 models in the EV sector in China, 11 of them are Chinese.*

The good news is, Tesla is battling, they're fighting. Their sales figures are very good. But Tesla is increasingly facing fierce competition from the home (Chinese) teams. The SOEs are in there, too, but their strength up until now has been their ability to manufacture at low cost.

***Fannin:* Which will dominate the Chinese auto market—SOEs or private enterprise?**

Dunne: We know that Xi Jinping wants the state to lead, to be the vanguard of the economy. And yet, the reality is that most of the innovation and creativity resides with these private entrepreneurs who are coming. That's a tension. How will that play out? That's to be determined.

***Fannin:* Is there going to be Chinese pushback against Tesla, given the US–China trade wars and tariffs?**

Dunne: It seems to be inevitable. Just look at General Motors. It was the poster child, arguably for the US. For many years, GM had a highly profitable joint venture with (state-owned) SAIC. Both parties were very happy. Other automakers, would say, 'Oh, God, if we could just have this SAIC-GM joint venture relationship, everything would be wonderful.' But now they're undergoing a major restructuring, and the word is that the joint venture will more than likely not be renewed when it expires in 2027. GM may or may not stay in the market.

Fannin: **What's the future for Detroit?**

Dunne: We're living on an island here in the US. In Detroit, GM is making good money. Everybody's getting a bonus. Unions are being paid. They're selling large trucks and SUVs to Americans, and when that's comfortable and inviting, then we don't look what's happening outside our borders. I'm from Detroit. I think it's very hard to change that culture you've built around manufacturing at the plant, putting together components in a car and doing it really well. *Elon has said, in the absence of tariffs, Chinese automakers would pretty much demolish most other legacy automakers around the world.*

Fannin: **So the only thing we can depend upon is tariffs?**

Dunne: Tariffs, to me, are a timeout.

Fannin: **What is the US doing with that timeout?**

Dunne: The Inflation Reduction Act has incentivized investment in batteries and battery supply chains, and electric vehicle production. We've seen more than $100 billion in investments and promised investments in the Battery Belt of the US. That's the good news. The tougher news is that, whereas China can channel demand to electrics and encourage it every day through subsidies and media, here in the US, we're definitely on the fence about buying electric vehicles. If we don't have the demand, then this $100 billion investment is just going to be, well, what for?

Fannin: **Which are more profitable, EVs or gas-powered vehicles?**

Dunne: Today, gas-powered vehicles are the source of profits. It's still less expensive to build a conventional vehicle than an electric. The main reason for that is the battery. Costs are coming down, but they're still at parity or slightly above gas-powered vehicles. If you don't have scale, and your costs are even and you've got a big battery that's expensive, then you don't enjoy any economies of scale. You have real cost problems. The Chinese, because they're selling 12 million EVs a year, have this scale so some of their companies can begin to make a profit.

Fannin: **How are the Japanese and Korean automakers faring in China?**

Dunne: They're definitely suffering, too, in China, just like other global automakers. It's like China time. Outside of China, the Japanese and Koreans have done a much better job of remaining competitive around the world. GM bet on China and the US—the big markets in the world for profits. But as China has gone, GM is shrinking in North America. It's a similar story for Ford and Stellantis. The Japanese and Koreans didn't make this mistake. They're present in most markets around the world, and understand they have to remain competitive there.

Fannin: **Can Chinese automakers compete in a global marketplace?**

Dunne: Today, you have world-class designers and engineers being hired from Europe and even Japan and Korea to come to China and work in these Chinese companies. It's not like when Korea or Japan relied entirely on their own homegrown talent to build up. The Chinese are saying, "We'll pay double, triple to hire these people, bring them to China, and we'll be world class." For example, BYD hired Wolfgang Egger from Audi. He's based in Shenzhen, where BYD headquarters are. Some of the designers are there, too, but many are also in Europe. He's got a global team of 600 designers, coming up with world-class designs. When it comes to manufacturing, the Chinese have embraced automation and robotics.

Fannin: **What's the biggest risk the US faces from China's gains in the automotive market?**

Dunne: The single biggest risk is that the Chinese do it faster and at lower cost.

Fannin: **How should the US respond?**

Dunne: China has always been aiming to be number one. But the US for much of the time is sort of taking a nap. You have this battle, but one of the sides is not really engaged.

CHAPTER 10

THE AGE OF DRONES AND ROBOTS

Drones and robots are increasingly useful in factories, residences, military operations, and even in everyday life. Chinese makers like DJI and Unitree are putting their stamp on owning a substantial share of these fast-evolving markets. Humanoid robots are coming!

Section I: Chinese Drones Take Over the Skies

Walking up Fifth Avenue in midtown Manhattan, a sleek, minimalist storefront selling electronic gadgets caught my eye. No, it wasn't Apple. Then, I spotted the logo above the entrance—DJI. While many consumers along this upscale stretch may not recognize the name, I knew it instantly as the world's leading drone maker from China. This is DJI's only store in the US—a showroom to display its cameras, drones, and handheld imaging devices. The bestseller? A $500 miniature vlogging camera with a built-in stabilizer, meant for shooting videos on the go.

DJI's presence on this main shopping thoroughfare is a sign of Chinese tech innovators continuing to go global in a bold way. The prime location, just steps from Trump Tower, is remarkable given the challenges this drone maker has faced over its Chinese origins. US investment and export restrictions, national security issues, and a looming ban have threatened its position. Yet, the privately owned Shenzhen-based company, short for Da-Jiang Innovations, has continued to soar.

The company revolutionized the drone industry in 2013 by inventing the Phantom, an easy-to-use, ready-to-fly model. Two years later came its model with a built-in livestreaming camera. Positioned as a premium consumer brand, DJI became known as the "Apple of drones," with snazzy marketing and designs. Its product names—Maven, Inspire, Spark, and Phantom—showcase creativity and ambition. Its diversification into an ecosystem of drones and related products speaks of Apple smarts. Its retail shops take a cue from Apple, with space for demonstrations, workshops, and videos. The company's futuristic skyscraper headquarters in Shenzhen, designed by renowned Foster & Partners (the architectural practice that created Apple's circular base in Silicon Valley) features cantilevered floors, gardens, twin towers connected by a sky bridge, and even a robot-fighting ring.

These bold moves reflect the vision of DJI's founder, Frank Wang (b. 1980), a press-shy product genius and tech tycoon who subscribes to Steve Jobs's approach: design the product first and let the market follow. At one point, speculation swirled that Apple might acquire DJI, as the iPhone maker mulled an entry into the consumer drone market. While that didn't occur, Apple had previously prominently displayed DJI's popular Phantom drones in its stores. Now, at Apple's Fifth Avenue location near Central Park, DJI products aren't displayed and only one item is in stock.

DJI has shifted its strategy to online sales today, at Amazon, Best Buy, Walmart, Alibaba's AliExpress, and DJI's own site. Many items sell out quickly and are out of stock. DJI has been having issues with getting stock to the US. One issue is increased tariffs on Chinese goods. The other is stricter US Customs Border and Protection Investigations, a governmental security audit, and a possible ban. DJI has put out a call asking for the government to do its best to attempt to find a security risk in its drones, believing it will pass the test with flying colors.[1]

Progress at a Price

Washington's concerns over Chinese surveillance have cast a shadow over DJI's success. Governmental scrutiny has focused on a security threat from use of DJI cameras, mapping technology, and infrared scans that could collect sensitive data and be shared with Chinese authorities. In 2020, the US Commerce Department barred American companies from exporting technology to DJI.[2] A year later, the Treasury Department banned US investments in DJI, accusing it of assisting the People's Liberation Army and using its drones to spy on Uyghur Muslims held in camps in Xinjiang province.[3] In addition, the Commerce Department has been considering new rules that would restrict or prohibit US use of drones or components produced or supplied by foreign adversaries, pinpointing China and Russia.[4]

Moreover, in 2017, the US Army discontinued use of DJI drones, and in 2020, the Interior Department grounded drones (except for emergencies) manufactured in China or made with Chinese components. Later, in 2022, after determining the potential security risks were low, the Interior Department eased that restriction but left in place rules about procuring foreign-made drones.[5]

Facing these formidable challenges, DJI has pushed back. The drone maker has lobbied against US bills to ban its drones, and fought against governmental warnings of DJI espionage and data theft. The company has reiterated a commitment to data security and has emphasized the usefulness of its products for small businesses ranging from real estate to agriculture. DJI has asserted that all its manufacturing occurs in Shenzhen or Malaysia—not in Xinjiang, where allegations of forced labor persist. In 2019, DJI opened an assembly line in California and introduced a Government Edition drone designed to keep data secured within the device and not transmitted wirelessly.[6]

Yet obstacles remain. DJI customers have complained about shipment delays, and DJI has responded that the US Customs and Border Protection is blocking some imports of its consumer drones.[7]

Shenzhen Valley Benefits

DJI is based in Shenzhen for a very good reason. This former fishing village that became the world's factory for Apple iPhone and Nike sneakers also designed and developed highly advanced technological products such as drones and other internet-connected devices. DJI's location in this Silicon Valley of China has afforded the company direct access to suppliers, raw materials, and a young, talent pool. DJI rose to dominance with a strong engineering bent and focus on innovation—one-quarter of its 14,000 employees work in research and development.

Proximity to designers and component suppliers lets DJI do rapid prototyping to find out what concepts work in practice, scrap those that don't work, and perfect those that do.

DJI can design and test its drones within one day, and ship them out with little time lost. This has given DJI a competitive advantage in cost of capital, manufacturing, and distribution.

From a startup in 2006, DJI has expanded to eight offices in key cities. Globally, it has 70 percent of the overall drone market and 90 percent of consumer drones sold, with a lineup of models for hobbyist aerial photography and videography. Drones are becoming increasingly popular and mainstream. Already a $73 billion market, drone sales are projected to grow 14.3 percent annually to 2030, with both consumer and enterprise segments increasing by double-digit gains.[8]

A catalyst for this growth is improved technology such as increased battery efficiency, enhanced imaging sensors, and AI-powered autonomous systems. Drones have grown in use for fighting wildfires, search-and-rescue missions, inspections of infrastructure and agriculture, or just as a hobby—flying them for fun. Drones can be fun, but also dangerous. For instance, there's a drone model that fits on the roof of a car and can be activated during a traffic jam to take flight and see what's blocking the road. And there are large drones or autonomous aerial vehicles made by China's EHang and Xpeng that can take off like a small passenger helicopter, controlled by a mobile app. China made headlines with a "drone mothership" innovation that could transport 100 UAVs (unmanned artillery vehicles), seemingly for defense purposes.[9]

Of the top 10 drone makers worldwide, China ranks up there with four, and DJI is by far in the lead.[10] But as geopolitical tensions have mounted around potential security risks from Chinese-made drones, now some non-Chinese drone alternatives are gaining in market segments. For instance, the US-made Skydio from Silicon Valley is gaining traction for enterprise applications like infrastructure inspections and public safety.

DJI stands out as the rare Chinese company that could ace a global market and leapfrog others by technological superiority, speed, efficiencies, and innovations, pointed out David Benowitz, head of research at industry analytics firm DroneAnalyst. I first met him at DJI offices in Shenzhen way back in 2018, when he was a cofounder of enterprise solutions at DJI. Having worked at DJI for four years and waited out the COVID pandemic from Shenzhen, he's recently moved to Seattle and also taken on a role as vice president of strategy and marketing for drone maker BRINC. Keeping a close eye on industry trends, he noted that the influence of DJI has expanded with several spin-offs founded by ex-DJI engineers such as Unitree, Bambulab, Ecoflow, and others. He further pointed out another key to its success: DJI has grown by diversifying its drone lineup into technology for electric bikes, autos, lidar, and portable power systems.

The increased scrutiny and geopolitical pressures have led DJI to reduce its presence at the annual Consumer Electronics Show in Las Vegas. By contrast, at the 2018 show, DJI had invited attendees to fly drones and displayed a full lineup in flight at its exhibit. More recently, DJI hasn't had its own branded booth but has demonstrated its products at a Qualcomm booth. This leading Chinese tech innovator still makes the trade press. News of the model DJI Flip, with a bunch of new features such as a larger battery and enhanced camera, was leaked right before the annual January 2025 show.

DJI Defeats GoPro's Drone

Over its short history, DJI has taken on mighty challenges and defeated rivals. One was Silicon Valley–based action camera maker GoPro. This well-known brand launched its drone Karma in 2016 only to quit the market two years later after failing to get uptake. GoPro was too late with a market entrant, and more than that, its drone did not measure up to DJI's lighter, smaller, and cheaper drone with a longer flight time. DJI also chased away another rival, 3D Robotics in Berkeley, California. The cofounders were prior *Wired* magazine editor Chris Anderson and Colin Guinn, former North American head of DJI who was embroiled in a dispute with founder Wang over credit for the success of the Phantom drone. Wang bought out Gunn's stake in DJI in 2013, shifted all operations to China, and reached $130 million in revenues that year, turning to profitability in 2014. In 2016, rival 3D Robotics quit making drones and transitioned to software.[11]

Meanwhile, DJI has continued to score with more funding. Its last known funding round of $1 billion in 2018 was at a mind-boggling valuation of $15 billion. Speculation about an IPO persists,[12] but Wang, who still holds a majority stake and is buying up shares from other investors, has kept his company's plans secretive.

That's the culture of DJI—private. DJI started out with angel investment from a family friend and progressed from there. The startup pulled in around $30 million at a valuation of $1.6 billion in January 2015 from Sequoia Capital China, then $75 million at an $8 billion valuation in May 2015 from Silicon Valley–based Accel Partners, the same firm that backed Facebook and Dropbox. One of its investors was New Horizon Capital, cofounded by Winston Wen, the son of former Chinese premier Wen Jiabao. The Chinese firm also has received funding from several state-backed investor groups. DJI has pointedly claimed state ownership is less than 6 percent of the company's shares.[13]

Visting DJI

Back in the relatively calmer geopolitical period of 2018, when I had a memorable visit to DJI in Shenzhen's sprawling Viseen Software Tech Park, I got a demo of its heavy-duty and lightweight drones flying high above the surrounding corporate buildings. I even got to fly one myself. Those drones whirl by like giant bumblebees but are actually hardworking aerial robots that can do surveillance and inspections for utilities, construction sites, airplanes, and trains from onboard cameras. Drones can also capture that perfect image of a wedding or graduation. They can have militaristic purposes too.

DJI's founder Wang hails from Hangzhou and is the son of a teacher and small businessowner. Wang had a dream of flying from when he was a kid, and he spent a good deal of his childhood building and flying model airplanes and wondering how to make a toy plane that wouldn't crash. While attending the Hong Kong University of Science and Technology as an engineering student in 2003, he got a research grant of $2,300 in 2005 to develop a drone. From his Hong Kong dorm room and with the help of his mentor Professor Li Zexiang, he formed an unmanned mini-helicopter flight control system, the seed of DJI in 2006.

Originally a hobby and a student project, DJI turned into a full-fledged business. DJI's Phantom drone that was introduced in early 2013 was the first mini copter that could be taken out of the box and assembled in one hour for flight, and without falling apart on its first crash. Soon, recreational drones became the latest fad, and Wang's fortunes soared.

Wang cracked the *Forbes* "Richest in Tech" list in 2017, at the age of 37, Asia's youngest tech billionaire, worth some $3.2 billion. The publicity-shy Wang with his circular glasses, tuft of chin stubble, and golf cap became the world's first drone billionaire. That wealth comes from Wang's substantial ownership of DJI shares and the company's profitability.

These are tall achievements for a 20-year-old company anywhere in the world. But for a Chinese tech giant weathering the stormy seas of US–China relations, the challenges ahead may be its toughest yet.

Section II: A Robotics Revolution in China

Robots are coming that can walk, dance, jump, converse, and even mimic a dog. Yet it's their ability to work on assembly lines, serve as caregivers and security patrols, fold the laundry, mop the floor, and deliver the mail that's fueling a robotics revolution.

China leads the world in industrial robots, with a record 1.7 million at work, and gains of nearly 300,000 annually in Chinese electronics and automotive factories. The US counts just 38,000 industrial robots.[14]

On the horizon (and eerily close) are so-called humanoid robots—mechanical creatures made to resemble humans. Powered by AI and sensors, these humanlike robots can do a bunch of complicated tasks real humans would rather avoid.

There's still some work to be done to perfect their motions so they move without bumping into things or falling. In what was billed as a showcase of China's cutting-edge technology, in April 2025, a half-marathon race in Beijing was held pitting humans against humanoid robots. It ended up being an embarrassment for developers as most of the humanoid robots stumbled, overheated, or failed to finish.[15]

Yet with technological advances, long-term prospects are good for these fascinating creatures. There's a growing need for them in factories due to a labor shortage. And demand for service robots in professional cleaning, hospitality and home care is also increasing.[16]

Again, it's China that is getting ahead in this emerging technology—just as with electric vehicles. China is leveraging its ability to mass produce at competitive prices, and proving its skills in innovating new capabilities of humanlike robots. There are more than 160 humanoid robot makers worldwide, and China has the most—60, followed by Europe and the US at 30.[17]

Please Mop That Up

Prices for humanoid robots vary widely depending upon features and use, ranging from $2,400 to $21,000 for personal home assistance or education models, from $30,000 to $100,000 for commercial use, and upward of $100,00 for high-end industrial models.

"The question of whether people are going to want to pay $20,000 for a humanoid robot to take care of them in their old age is another issue. Certainly, humanoid robots have lots of potential use cases, and China is going to be the country that produces those at scale and cost, not the US. I mean that's not even a contest," observed tech consultant Triolo.

Two Chinese robotics startups, Hong Kong–listed UBTech and Alibaba-backed Unitree, are emerging as dominant players in this sector in China. In the US, key contender Boston Dynamics makes a humanoid robot designed for search-and-rescue missions, and recently teamed up with Nvidia to use its AI technology to improve dexterity and locomotion for a next generation of humanoid robots. Boston Dynamics also has a four-legged mobile robot, Spot, priced at $74,500, developed in 2020 for the industrial market—useful for construction sites, factory floors, and monitoring remote or hazardous environments. Tesla's humanoid robot project Optimus has gotten in the running too. Elon Musk has vowed to have his near-six-foot tall Optimus bot for sale by 2026, ready to mow the lawn or clean the kitchen, and priced below $20,000.[18]

China's tech titan companies see the potential of humanoid robots, too, and also are venturing into developing and producing them. Alibaba's fintech affiliate Ant Group has formed a subsidiary to invest in Mindtree and its cousins, as Jack Ma signals: "AI will bring a greater era."[19] Lei Jun, founder and CEO of Chinese consumer electronics Xiaomi, unveiled the company's first full-size humanoid robot, CyberOne, in Beijing in 2022, and may be about to mass produce it. Tencent has been investing in this industry since 2018 and has capitalized UBTech. EV makers BYD and Xpeng, are betting on humanoid robots, too, and are well equipped to have a head start on producing and developing them thanks to overlapping sensor and algorithmic technologies that guide movements. Then there's Shenzhen-based Pudu Robotics, a maker of robotic vacuums and mops that also now is making a full-size, sensor-equipped D9 delivery robot that can walk-run 4.5mph and carry loads up to 44 pounds.[20] As a sign of where this is going, Pudu Robotics has recently expanded its training and demonstration base in Santa Clara and opened a fulfillment center in New Jersey for distribution.

As progress in AI accelerates and investment increases, analysts predict this robotics market will reach $38 billion by 2035,[21] up by more than sixfold from an earlier estimate of $6 billion. Goldman Sachs Research has pointed out that robotics development has sped up by AI models that can train themselves without needing human engineers to manually code them. Morgan Stanley has predicted the AI robots could fill a labor gap, reaching 40,000 by 2030, and climbing to 63 million by 2050.[22] A drop in manufacturing costs of humanoid robots is leading to larger-scale and faster commercialization.

Pepper and Sophia, Come Back!

Not all AI human bots have been successful. Japan's SoftBank pioneered personal robotics in 2014 with Pepper Robot, a retail store assistant and home companion. But SoftBank stopped producing Pepper in 2020, facing losses and lack of demand.

It was an attractive humanoid named Sophia that first captivated the public in 2016 when she appeared at the South by Southwest festival in Austin. Created by Hanson Robotics, a Hong Kong–based startup founded by former Disney imagineer David Hanson, Sophia was originally funded by China's tech investor AngelVest Group in Shanghai. The vision was grand: build robots in Chinese factories to assist with services like elderly care. But what happened instead was that Sophia was made manually and became a "showbot"—a traveling spectacle at conferences and events around the world. I witnessed her appearance firsthand at a gathering of US–China dealmakers in New York City. "That was the bread and butter of how the company made money for several years," said David Chen, cofounder of AngelVest. "But that obviously has its limitations."

A second endeavor, the shoebox-sized Professor Einstein robot, was produced in Shenzhen but never reached the market. "There were missed opportunities that prevented the company from making these breakthroughs," said Chen. One internal debate was over artistic direction versus commercialization. "If you just have the artistry without the business part," Chen noted, "then it is just art."

I recall first seeing these humanoid robots at the Consumer Electronics Show in Las Vegas, and being mesmerized by them. That was several years ago. Today, their appeal extends beyond novelty. They steal the show for becoming more functional, more intelligent, and more integral for industrial and consumer use.

Robots Take to Work

Perhaps there's no surprise that China is the world's leading producer of robotics and the largest market for industrial robots, accounting for more than half installed at factories globally—and that's up from 14 percent a decade earlier.[23] But while Chinese robotic producers have been gaining, they remained, as "fast followers, competing on lower costs while still relying on Western innovation," the Information Technology and Innovation Foundation (ITIF) found. Western companies hold an edge in AI software, while Asia's manufacturing infrastructure and wide supply chain provide an advantage for producing lower-cost hardware at scale.[24]

The ITIF report goes on to note that the "United States invented robotics, but like so many other industries, it lost leadership to foreign competitors, in part because companies lacked patient capital. Other nations were willing to invest for the long haul. Today, the leading robotics producers are in Germany, Japan, and Switzerland, while China is working vigorously to catch up."[25]

To wit, China leads the world in robotics patents, accounting for 35 percent of the worldwide total. In another telling indicator, ITIF found that, of the top 20 organizations filing for patents, the US had none and China held seven.[26] Moreover, a Morgan Stanley report noted that China leads the world in the number of humanoid mentions in global patent filings.[27]

China Loves Humanoids

Seeing the potential, China has prioritized adoption of robotics in manufacturing and is also pushing humanoid robots as a new engine of growth, aiming for mass production in 2025 and world leadership by 2027.[28] In China, almost three-quarters of production is done by automation and machinery. Robots, as has been noted, have no real problem in handling "dangerous, dirty and dull jobs."[29]

The Chinese government is "not leaving humanoid robots to market forces alone," newsletter *TechBuzz China* noted. Similar to its strategy for electric vehicles, Beijing is pouring in resources, investing heavily in core technologies, securing supply chain dominance, and driving costs down through large-scale manufacturing, founding editor Rui Ma concluded. Cities and provinces have introduced policies to accelerate the industry's growth, with ambitious production targets laid out by Beijing and Shanghai over the next two years. The Beijing municipal government recently announced a $1.4 billion robotics fund. The Chinese city of Dongguan has emerged as a hub for state-backed research institutes and robotics companies.

A Threat from China's Robots

This aggressive expansion has sparked concerns in the US about maintaining technological leadership and protecting its turf. Oliver Mitchell, a robotics expert and partner at ff Venture Capital in New York City, observed:

China has been a low-cost manufacturing hub for decades, while the United States leads in creative vision for technology startups and global workflow trends. There would be no DeepSeek if Open AI wasn't first, and likewise no Unitree without Tesla's Optimus. To prevent a future DJI takeover for the humanoid space, the US government and domestic manufacturers must be laser focused on securing our supply chain for AI and robot IP within our borders. This is not only about commerce, but national security.

In Washington, DC, policymakers are taking notice of China's AI-enabled humanoid robots that have lifelike characteristics. An opinion piece in *The Wall Street Journal* by Senator Katie Britt and Under Secretary of State Jacob Helberg (a former Palantir Technologies senior adviser and commissioner for the US–China Economic and Security Review) warned about this next threat from China and the need for the US to develop critical technology independent of China. They called on Congress to ban Chinese imports of these robots that can blend in seamlessly into everyday life and pose a potential threat to personal data security.[30] They also have raised concerns about their usage in surveillance and espionage.

Meanwhile, US export bans on Nvidia chips to China threaten to slow the country's progress. Chinese robotics makers can seek alternative sources or develop domestic chips, but it's hard to match Nvidia's sophisticated processing capabilities, particularly for tasks requiring vision coordination and precise movement.

100 Million Robot Program

But China is determined as ever. Only China could launch more than 3,400 robotics startups as part of a "100 Million Robot" initiative.[31] Despite obstacles, Chinese humanoid robotic makers are gaining ground, competing against industry leaders such as Tesla's robotics assistant Optimus for vehicles and Boston Dynamics's cutting-edge industrial robots.

Among these fierce challengers is UBTech, founded in Shenzhen in 2012 as a specialist in companion and service robots. Its flagship model, Walker X, is highly mobile and dexterous, able to open doors and carry objects. UBTech was one of the first to commercialize humanoid robots, and within 10 years of its start, held more than 1,800 robotic and AI patents, including 380 overseas patents. Initially backed in 2015 by Qiming Venture Partners, the startup secured $820 million in funding led by Tencent in 2018 before going public in Hong Kong in 2023 and raising $130 million. At its listing ceremony, company chairman Zhou Jian struck a ceremonial gong—alongside Walker S, the firm's newest industrial humanoid robot.

Another prime contender, Unitree Robotics, was founded in 2016 in Hangzhou by former DJI engineer Wang Xingxing and is being touted for the potential to revolutionize robotics—like DeepSeek has upturned AI. Unitree's robots are tough, agile, and waterproof, and these machines can climb stairs, carry heavy loads, and do gymnastics. Unitree recently made a splash by debuting its H1 humanoid robot dancing on stage at a televised Lunar New Year Festival. Its first robot dog, the Go1, was introduced in 2021 as a consumer model priced at $1,600 and was designed to have similar features to Boston Dynamics' popular Spot, but smaller and much cheaper (and a quieter bark?). Unitree has loads of financing. In addition to funding from Alibaba, Unitree obtained capital from Beijing and Shanghai municipal funds, venture units of Chinese smartphone maker Xiaomi and delivery super app Meituan, as well as VCs Lightspeed China Partners and Matrix Partners China. As a sign of its significance to China's economy and private enterprise, Unitree's CEO was seated in a front row among the country's top tech business executives (including DeepSeek) at that early 2025 summit called by Chinese leader Xi Jinping.

On social media, Unitree's humanoid robots have captured millions of views for their humanlike skills. For example, the Unitree G1 Bionic, standing over four feet tall, weighing more than 77 pounds, boasting a two-hour battery life, and running at a speed of 4.4mph, has been described as the ultimate jogging partner. But with a $16,000 price tag, as one TikTok podcaster quipped, "Are we ready to share the street with robots?"[32]

As these machines become more advanced, their presence in daily life is shifting from futuristic fantasy to reality. Humanoid robots are clearly no longer the stuff of science fiction. They are here, and they are only getting smarter.

It sounds like China.

AFTERWORD

The gap between the US and China is widening over technology leadership but not always with America ahead.

How much longer can Silicon Valley claim title as the world's technology, innovation, and venture capital center?

We are at a crossroads where China continues to gain despite considerable pushback from the US. The blocks on US technology penetrating China are only making this chief rival more self-sufficient, not needing American knowhow, and keen to develop its own standards.

The days when US–China cross-border investment and collaboration worked well are gone. California's Sand Hill Road investors funded China's startups that often copied the best US ideas and grew up to be tech titans with their own inventions. Despite Chinese government crackdowns on their power and influence, China's entrepreneurial spirit wasn't crushed. Titans and startups alike kept coming.

The US can no longer dismiss or ignore China's Silicon Dragon. Now it's considered a threat. Conflict over superpower status has caused both sides to go their own way. When the Valley's venture capitalists were restricted from investing in cutting-edge China tech, the gap was filled mostly by large state-backed funds. When the US limited investments and advanced technology to China, the Chinese found workarounds.

This split is detrimental to advancements for the world's future in many broad sectors—communications, commerce, artificial intelligence, transportation, and production. China is catching up or surpassing the US in all these areas, and growing its own.

The Mainland's gains are driven by state control that dictates national priorities of core technologies that matter most, like semiconductors and AI.

The CHIPS and Science Act of 2022, a $52 billion US governmental program to support America's chip industry, was a positive sign that the US needed to do something big and urgently to rebuild our industrial base. It was the largest US technology and industrial policy program in modern history. But it was dwarfed by China's "Big Fund" for semiconductors that totals $145.5 billion.

And while gains are being made in reshoring factories to American soil and securing critical supply chains, results from pushing for more new energy initiatives and funding chips plants have become uncertain, given recent policy changes and budget cuts.

Intel was awarded nearly $8 billion in direct funding from the government along with a 25 percent investment tax credit to support its plans to invest more than $100 billion across four states, $28 billion going to build two chip factories in New Albany, Ohio, near Columbus. Slated to be the largest semiconductor manufacturing site of the next decade, it's located on more than 900 acres in central Ohio's agricultural lands. I've seen the construction underway along Route 70 on my regular driving trips from New York City to my hometown, Lancaster, 34 miles southeast of the site. Interestingly, this new techie area became known as Silicon Heartland, the title of my 2023 book about transformation of the Rust Belt into a Tech Belt.

It saddens me to know that funding is being cut for this revival of the Heartland, and progress is being delayed. The government's recent 10 percent stake in Intel might help but it's a controversial move that might not yield the results we need.

Meanwhile, chipmakers TSMC, Samsung, and Micron Technology are investing billions to build semiconductor plants and create thousands of jobs over the next few years in the US, with government support. But most chip production could remain in Taiwan, a national security risk.

If all these investment commitments do hold up, the US would be on track to produce nearly 30 percent of leading-edge chips by 2032. But that's a big IF.[1]

Geopolitics has become a major force that is shaping technology innovation and investment worldwide. Nowhere is this more pronounced than now in the US and China, from chips to electric vehicles to robotics and drones to batteries, which are already increasingly being led by China. As tech continues to evolve, new battlelines could be drawn. In an ideal world, we would compete and collaborate side by side. Innovation would benefit worldwide.

Acknowledgments

This is not my first book. But it's the first time for a second edition.

Therefore some people who were thanked the first time around get double billing now.

I wish to thank those who took time from their busy schedules to do interviews with me for this book. Some of them were interviewed twice and had follow-up questions.

Thanks goes to Gary Rieschel of Qiming Venture, Hurst Lin of DCM, James Mi of Lightspeed China, who all appeared in the initial version. And to newcomers who were quoted liberally: Paul Triolo of DGA-Albright Stone Group, Isaac Stone Fish of Strategy Risks, Ker Kibbs of Foresight Group, Craig Allen of The Cohen Group, Michael Dunne of Dunne Insights, Michael Zakkour of 5 New Digital, China tech observer Rui Ma, Mitch Presnick of Harvard's Fairbank Center and Super 8 Hotels China, Oliver Mitchell of ff Venture, AI agent entrepreneur Frank Yu, David Benowitz of BRINC, and Silicon Valley tech investors Purvi Gandhi and Stella Yin and others who were sounding boards. Special thanks to my longtime editor/agent Leah Spiro, former *AVCJ* publisher Dan Schwartz, and China pro Jim McGregor for your insights. An extra-special thanks to John for all the walks 'n' talks, the clips, and joys. My thanks to Jonathan Shipley of Hachette Book Group in London for contacting me about writing this second edition, and following through well with the team: Iain Campbell, Abigail Chatterjee, Robert Tuesley Anderson, Melissa Carl, and more.

Writing a topical, international book—especially one involving China—requires a certain dedication, perseverance, and energy level. You have to go to China to write about it! I wish to thank my husband, and my parents who raised me to work hard and dream big. They may not have encouraged me to take so many risks as I have, traveling to and from China and elsewhere numerous times on my own. But it's worked out so far.

I wish to thank all those who have supported my own entrepreneurial career. Special thanks to David Kaufman of Nixon Peabody, Curtis Mo of DLA Piper, Lawrence Tang of InvestHK, Jessica Ng of Cyberport, Thomas Chou of Morrison & Foerster, Lili Zheng of Deloitte, John Oden and Ben Stein of Alliance Bernstein and the China US Business Alliance, Lilly Huang of Citi, and Harry Edelson of the China Investment Group plus core members of this group I now lead including John Allen, Steve Schuster, William Brothers, David Dempsey, Michael Silver, Elizabeth Wang, and Ming Zhong as well as fellow entrepreneurs Sidney Armani and David Cao. Not forgetting several Silicon Dragon members for many years: Henry Tang, Robert Haddock, Jason Ma, Sharon Yang, Michael Jaliman, Rosemary Coates, Hal Kellman, James Zhang and Jin Zhao.

And thanks, too, of course, to the many venture capitalists who've appeared on my *Ask a VC* online show over the past five years. One more I cannot forget: Leading Authorities for arranging several speaking appearances.

Can I say thank you to libraries? Okay! I spend too much time in them, but grateful for the environment around books and the silent company of others in front of their laptops and periodicals. Shout out to great libraries in North Stamford and New Canaan, Connecticut, and Burlingame, California, which also happens to have the best little café in this town. By the way, this Silicon Valley gem is named after nineteenth-century American diplomat Anson Burlingame, who became China's envoy to the West, fostering early diplomatic ties between the US and China. Kind of fitting that I make this pleasant place to write one of my homes.

Rebecca A. Fannin
Fall 2025

Notes

Chapter 1

1. Zijing Wu and Michael Acton, Nvidia plans Shanghai research centre in new commitment to China, *Financial Times*, May 16, 2025, https://www.ft.com/content/c886a4c0-da75-4ea7-8230-6ffd18815fa4
2. William Alan Reinsch and Jack Whitney, Silicon Island: Assessing Taiwan's importance to US economic growth and security, Center for Strategic & International Studies, January 10, 2025, https://www.csis.org/analysis/silicon-island-assessing-taiwans-importance-us-economic-growth-and-security
3. Ardi Janjeva, Seoin Baek, and Andy Sellars, China's quest for semiconductor self-sufficiency, Center for Emerging Technology and Security, Alan Turing Institute, December 4, 2024, https://cetas.turing.ac.uk/publications/chinas-quest-semiconductor-self-sufficiency
4. Dick Kramlich passed away in early 2025.
5. Ta-lin Hsu passed away in 2024, https://www.committee100.org/in-memoriam/ta-linhsu/
6. Emerging resilience in the semiconductor supply, Semiconductor Industry Association, Boston Consulting Group, May 2024, https://www.semiconductors.org/emerging-resilience-in-the-semiconductor-supply-chain/
7. Global fab equipment investment to hit $110B in 2025, *Control Engineering*, March 31, 2025, https://www.controleng.com/global-fab-equipment-investment-to-hit-110b-in-2025/
8. Stephen Ezell, How innovative is China in semiconductors?, Information Technology & Innovation Foundation, August 19, 2024, https://itif.org/publications/2024/08/19/how-innovative-is-china-in-semiconductors/

9. Gracelin Baskaran, What China's ban on rare earths processing technology exports means, Center for Strategic and International Studies, January 8, 2024, https://www.csis.org/analysis/what-chinas-ban-rare-earths-processing-technology-exports-means
10. Global fab equipment investment to hit $110B in 2025, *Control Engineering*, March 31, 2025, https://www.controleng.com/global-fab-equipment-investment-to-hit-110b-in-2025/
11. Stephen Ezell, How innovative is China in semiconductors?, Information Technology & Innovation Foundation, August 19, 2024, https://itif.org/publications/2024/08/19/how-innovative-is-china-in-semiconductors/
12. Charles Roullet, DeepSeek isn't taking VC money yet, *TechCrunch*, March 10, 2025, https://techcrunch.com/2025/03/10/deepseek-isnt-taking-vc-money-yet-here-are-3-reasons-why/
13. Keith Bradsher, China halts critical exports as trade war intensifies, *New York Times*, April 13, 2025, https://www.nytimes.com/2025/04/13/business/china-rare-earths-exports.html
.14 Global energy investment set to rise to $3.3 trillion in 2025; International Energy Agency, June 5, 2025, https://www.iea.org/news/global-energy-investment-set-to-rise-to-3-3-trillion-in-2025-amid-economic-uncertainty-and-energy-security-concerns
15. Aiqun Yu, Sophie Lu, Kasandra O'Malia, and Shradhey Prasad, China continues to lead the world in wind and solar, *Global Energy Monitor*, July 2024, https://globalenergymonitor.org/report/china-continues-to-lead-the-world-in-wind-and-solar-with-twice-as-much-capacity-under-construction-as-the-rest-of-the-world-combined/
16 World Robotics, Industrial Robots, International Federation of Robotics, https://ifr.org/wr-industrial-robots/
17 World Robotics 2024 presentation, International Federation of Robotics, September 24, 2024, https://ifr.org/ifr-press-releases/news/record-of-4-million-robots-working-in-factories-worldwide
18 Caiwei Chen, China's EV giants are betting big on humanoid robots, *MIT Technology Review*, February 14, 2025, https://www.technologyreview.com/2025/02/14/1111920/chinas-electric-vehicle-giants-pivot-humanoid-robots/
19 Britney Nguyen, Quartz: The top 10 countries in the world for computing power, January 6, 2025, https://tech.yahoo.com/computing/articles/top-10-countries-world-computing-100000736.html; Top 500 The List, *List Statistics*, November 2024, https://www.top500.org/statistics/list/
20. Alan Bradley, China achieves quantum supremacy claim, *Live Science*, March 13, 2025, https://www.livescience.com/technology/computing/

china-achieves-quantum-supremacy-claim-with-new-chip-1-quadrillion-times-faster-than-the-most-powerful-supercomputers

21. Lizzi Lee, China's quiet DeepSeek moment in biotech, *Asia Society*, March 15, 2025, https://asiasociety.org/video/chinas-quiet-deepseek-moment-biotech-rapid-rise-potential-risks-and-global-implications?page=110
22. Minhua Chu, China Biopharma Tracker 2024, *Pharma DJ*, January 13, 2025, https://www.pharmadj.com/en/article/1878614257145294850
23. Charting the Future of Biotechnology, National Security Commission on Emerging Biotechnology, April 2025, https://www.biotech.senate.gov/wp-content/uploads/2025/04/NSCEB-Full-Report-%E2%80%93-Digital-%E2%80%934.28.pdf
24. What is biotechnology, and how will it shape America's future?, National Security Commission on Emerging Biotechnology, April 2025, https://www.biotech.senate.gov/final-report/chapters/introduction/
25. Charting the future of biotechnology, National Security Commission on Emerging Biotechnology, April 2025, https://www.biotech.senate.gov/wp-content/uploads/2025/04/NSCEB-Full-Report-%E2%80%93-Digital-%E2%80%934.28.pdf. The congressional committee, recognizing China's ascent in biotechnology, has recommended ways to make the "US innovate faster and slow China down," such as an investment fund for US tech startups and restrictions on US capital to Chinese development of biotechnologies that threaten national security.
26. Justin McCurry, Scientist who gene-edited babies is back in lab and "proud" of past work despite jailing, *The Guardian*, April 1, 2024, https://www.theguardian.com/science/2024/apr/01/crispr-cas9-he-jiankui-genome-gene-editing-babies-scientist-back-in-lab
27. Genevieve Donnellon-May, How China's AI push in agritech is changing global trade flows, *South China Morning Post*, April 27, 2025, https://www.scmp.com/opinion/china-opinion/article/3307824/how-chinas-ai-push-agritech-changing-global-trade-flows
28. Pascal Coppens, China's next big boom: AgriTech and FoodTech, *YouTube*, 2022, https://www.youtube.com/watch?v=sAUk8E97-UE
29. Trends in the electric car industry, Global EV Outlook 2025, International Energy Agency, April 2025, https://www.iea.org/reports/global-ev-outlook-2025/executive-summary
30. James Bickerton, How US high-speed rail compares to China's, *Newsweek*, May 19, 2024, https://www.newsweek.com/how-us-high-speed-rail-plan-compares-chinas-1902160

31. Liu Mingtai and Zhou Huiying, CRRC unveils breakthrough hydrogen-powered urban train, *China Daily*, March 22, 2024.
32. Hongyang Cui, Ruichen Ma and Yini Liu, Charging up China's transition to electric vehicles, International Council on Clean Transportation; January 31, 2024, https://theicct.org/publication/charging-up-china-transition-to-ev-jan24/
33. Global EV Outlook 2025, International Energy Agency, May 14, 2025, https://www.iea.org/reports/global-ev-outlook-2025/electric-vehicle-charging
34. Chengyi Lin, The Chinese EV maker that made battery swapping work, *INSEAD Knowledge*, August 1, 2024, https://knowledge.insead.edu/strategy/chinese-ev-company-made-battery-swapping-work
35. Dylan Butts, China's CATL claims to beat BYD's EV battery record, *CNBC*, April 22, 2025, https://www.cnbc.com/2025/04/22/chinas-catl-claims-to-beat-byds-ev-battery-record-with-longer-range-on-a-5-minute-charge.html
36. Rebecca Fannin, Crash of China bike-sharing startup, *Forbes*, March 8, 2019, https://www.forbes.com/sites/rebeccafannin/2019/03/08/crash-of-china-bike-sharing-startup-ofo-costs-leading-vcs-big-time/
37. Matthew P. Funaiole, Brian Hart, and Aidan Powers-Riggs, China dominates the ship-building industry, Center for Strategic & International Studies, March 25, 2025, https://www.csis.org/analysis/china-dominates-shipbuilding-industry
38. Ziwen Zhao, China's Tiangong space station research aims to break technology choke points, *South China Morning Post*, December 31, 2024, https://www.scmp.com/news/china/science/article/3292844/chinas-tiangong-space-station-research-aims-break-technology-choke-points
39. Venture capital data, Preqin customized research, December 2024.
40. China to invest 1 trillion yuan in robotics and high-tech industries, International Federation of Robotics, March 25, 2025, https://ifr.org/ifr-press-releases/news/china-to-invest-1-trillion-yuan-in-robotics-and-high-tech-industries
41. The Midas List: the world's best venture capital investors in 2025, *Forbes*, May 27, 2025, https://www.forbes.com/lists/midas/
42. CB Insights, The complete list of unicorn companies, January 2025, https://www.cbinsights.com/research-unicorn-companies
43. Global unicorn index 2024; Hurun Research, https://www.hurun.net/en-us/info/detail?num=9K1G2SK5X7CX#:~:text=By%20city%2C%20San%20Francisco%20led,were%20IPOs%20and%206%20acquisitions

44. Hurun Future Unicorns Global Gazelles Index 2024, Hurun Research, January 8, 2025, https://www.hurun.net/en-US/Info/Detail?num=GCIFXN4SLF2V
45. CB Insights, The complete list of unicorn companies, January 2025, https://www.cbinsights.com/research-unicorn-companies
46. The Crunchbase unicorn board, *Crunchbase*, June 6, 2025, https://news.crunchbase.com/unicorn-company-list/
47. Use of WIPO's global IP registries for patents, trademarks and designs grew in 2024, World Intellectual Property Organization, March 17, 2025, https://www.wipo.int/pressroom/en/articles/2025/article_0003.html;IP Facts and Figures, WIPO Statistics Database, March 2025, https://www.wipo.int/en/ipfactsandfigures/patents; WIPO Press Room, March 17, 2025, https://www.wipo.int/pressroom/en/articles/2025/article_0003.html
48. WIPO IP Facts and Figures 2024, World Intellectual Property Organization, 2024, https://www.wipo.int/edocs/pubdocs/en/wipo-pub-943-2024-en-wipo-ip-facts-and-figures-2024.pdf
49. Trelysa Long, China is catching up in R&D, Information Technology & Innovation Foundation, April 9, 2025, https://itif.org/publications/2025/04/09/china-catching-up-rd-may-have-already-pulled-ahead/
50. Arjun Kharpal, Huawei launches its own operating system on smartphones, *CNBC*, June 2, 2021; https://www.cnbc.com/2021/06/02/huawei-harmonyos-operating-system-launched-on-smartphone-smartwatch.html
51. Liza Lin and Raffaele Huang, Huawei develops new chip seeking to match Nvidia, *The Wall Street Journal*, April 28, 2025, https://www.wsj.com/tech/chinas-huawei-develops-new-ai-chip-seeking-to-match-nvidia-8166f606
52. Juan Pedro Tomas, China claims world's first 6G field test network, *RCR Wireless News*, July 15, 2024, https://www.rcrwireless.com/20240715/featured/china-claims-world-first-field-test-network-6g-communications#:~:text=China%20aims%20to%20start%20commercializing,for%205G%20and%206G%20services
53. Anne Neuberger, China Is still winning the battle for 5G—and 6G, *Foreign Affairs*, July/August 2025, https://www.foreignaffairs.com/united-states/china-still-winning-battle-5g-and-6g
54. Internet Services in China, Market Research Report, 2015-2030, IBISWorld, https://www.ibisworld.com/china/industry/internet-services/805/
55. Broadband fact sheet, Pew Research Center, November 13, 2024, https://www.pewresearch.org/internet/fact-sheet/internet-broadband/

56. Sunil Gill, How many people own smartphones in the world?, *Priori Data*, January 1, 2025, https://perioridata.com/data/smartphone-stats/
57. Mobile fact sheet, Pew Research Center, November 13, 2024, https://www.pewresearch.org/internet/fact-sheet/mobile/
58. John Engen, Lessons from a mobile payments revolution, *American Banker*, https://www.americanbanker.com/news/why-chinas-mobile-payments-revolution-matters-for-us-bankers
59. Evelyn Cheng, Chinese livestreamers can rake in billions of dollars in hours, *CNBC*, November 16, 2021, https://www.cnbc.com/2021/11/16/chinese-livestreamers-can-rake-in-billions-of-dollars-in-hours-how-long-will-it-last.html
60. 2024–2025, Best global universities rankings, *US News & World Report*, June 24, 2024, https://www.usnews.com/education/best-global-universities
61. National Science Board, Science & engineering indicators, *The State of US Science & Engineering 2024*, https://ncses.nsf.gov/pubs/nsb20243
62. The Pritzker Architecture Prize, The Hyatt Foundation, March 4, 2025, https://www.pritzkerprize.com/laureates/liu-jiakun
63. Nobel Prizes by Country, World Population Review, 2025, https://worldpopulationreview.com/country-rankings/nobel-prizes-by-country
64. World's Billionaire List, The Richest in 2025, *Forbes*, April 13, 2025, https://www.forbes.com/billionaires/;https://www.forbes.com/sites/sylvanlebrun/2025/04/01/the-countries-with-the-most-billionaires-2025/
65. The 2025 billionaires breakdown, *Addis Insight*, April 4, 2025, https://www.addisinsight.net/2025/04/04/the-2025-billionaires-breakdown-tech-titans-finance-moguls-and-the-sectors-shaping-global-wealth/#google_vignette; The Richest People in Tech, *Forbes*, 2017 ranking, https://www.forbes.com/richest-in-tech/list/#tab:overall_country:China; Jane Ho and Yue Wang, China's richest 100, *Forbes*, November 6, 2024, https://www.forbes.com/lists/china-billionaires/
66. Daniel Liberto, Biggest companies in the world by market cap, *Investopia*, October 16, 2024, https://www.investopedia.com/biggest-companies-in-the-world-by-market-cap-5212784
67. Loren Grush, Eric Johnson, and Katie Roof, SpaceX valuation jumps to about $350 billion in insider deal, *Bloomberg News*, December 11, 2024, https://www.bloomberg.com/news/articles/2024-12-10/spacex-share-sale-is-said-to-value-company-at-about-350-billion
68. History.com editors, 1969 Moon landing, *History.com*, August 23, 2018, https://www.history.com/articles/moon-landing-1969

69. Rob Smith, IBM created world's first smartphone, World Economic Forum, March 13, 2018, https://www.weforum.org/stories/2018/03/remembering-first-smartphone-simon-ibm/

Chapter 2

1. Alizila staff, AliViews, *Alizila*, May 23, 2024, https://www.alizila.com/aliviews-alibaba-joe-tsai-eddie-wu-2024-letter-shareholders/
2. Rebecca Fannin, Facebook changes to be more like WeChat, *Forbes*, March 3, 2019; https://www.forbes.com/sites/rebeccafannin/2019/03/08/facebook-changes-to-be-more-like-wechat-are-part-of-copy-from-china-trend/
3. About Baidu, Products & Services, https://ir.baidu.com/Baidu-Core
4. Alibaba Group, Quick View, *DBS Treasures*, February 2025, https://www.dbs.com.hk/treasures/aics/stock-coverage/templatedata/article/equity/data/en/DBSV/012014/9988_HK.xml
5. Jeffrey Towson, Eddie Wu's Alibaba, *Tech Strategy*, January 16, 2025, https://jefftowson.com/membership_content/eddie-wus-alibaba-the-rise-of-an-ai-first-ecommerce-empire-tech-strategy/
6. Phil Serafino and Henry Ren, China tech is the comeback story of the year, *Bloomberg*, February 21, 2025, https://www.bloomberg.com/news/newsletters/2025-02-21/china-tech-is-the-comeback-story-of-the-year

Chapter 3

1. Casey Hall, Food delivery giant Meituan defies China consumer pullback with revenue beat, *Reuters*, August 28, 2024, https://www.reuters.com/technology/chinese-food-delivery-giant-meituan-beats-quarterly-revenue-estimates-2024-11-29/
2. Lai Lin Thomala, *Statista*, February 12, 2025, https://www.statista.com/statistics/910787/china-monthly-active-users-on-leading-news-apps/. Tencent News has 356 million monthly active users.
3. TikTok CEO Shou Chew's opening statement—Senate Judiciary Committee Hearing, January 31, 2024, https://newsroom.tiktok.com/en-us/opening-statement-senate-judiciary-committee-hearing
4. Joyce Guevarra and Neel Hiteshbhai Bharucha, China's ByteDance leads world's largest unicorns, *S&P Global*, March 10, 2025, https://www.spglobal.com/market-intelligence/en/news-insights/articles/2025/3/chinas-bytedance-leads-worlds-largest-unicorns-87731476

5. The CCP's investors, The Select Committee on the Strategic Competition between the US and the Chinese Communist Party, February 8, 2024, https://selectcommitteeontheccp.house.gov/sites/evo-subsites/selectcommitteeontheccp.house.gov/files/evo-media-document/2024-02-08%20-%20VC%20Report%20-%20FINAL.pdf
6. Regina Abrami, William Kirby, and F. Warren McFarlan, Why China can't innovate, *Harvard Business Review*, March 2014, https://hbr.org/2014/03/why-china-cant-innovate
7. Myths and facts, TikTok U.S. data security, https://usds.tiktok.com/usds-myths-vs-facts
8. Jeff Fromm, TikTok isn't the only social media channel available to Gen Z, *Forbes*, January 16, 2025, https://www.forbes.com/sites/jefffromm/2025/01/16/tiktok-isnt-the-only-social-media-channel-available-to-gen-z/
9. Luxuan Wang, A closer look at Americans' experiences with news on TikTok, *Pew Research*, January 17, 2025, https://www.pewresearch.org/short-reads/2025/01/17/a-closer-look-at-americans-experiences-with-news-on-tiktok/
10. Devan Burris, How TikTok Shop became the fastest-growing social media shopping platform, *CNBC Video*, March 30, 2025, https://www.cnbc.com/video/2025/03/30/how-tiktok-shop-became-the-fastest-growing-social-media-shopping-platform.html
11. Video, How TikTok's algorithm figures you out, *The Wall Street Journal*, July 21, 2021, https://www.youtube.com/watch?v=nfczi2cI6Cs
12. Sarah Jackson, *Business Insider*, March 26, 2025, https://www.businessinsider.com/tiktok-bytedance-founder-zhang-yiming-net-worth-2024-10#zhang-has-become-a-billionaire-owing-to-the-success-of tiktok-and-byte-dance-more-broadly-10; Zhang Yiming profile, *Forbes*, May 4, 2025, https://www.forbes.com/profile/zhang-yiming/
13. Rebecca A. Fannin, *Tech Titans of China*, John Murray Press, an imprint of Nicholas Brealey Publishing, 2019.
14. Liza Lin and Yoko Kubota, TikTok parent's founder Zhang to step down as CEO, *The Wall Street Journal*, May 20, 2021, https://www.wsj.com/articles/bytedance-founder-zhang-yiming-to-step-down-as-ceo-11621478797
15. Ben Jiang, China's hottest AI bot? *South China Morning Post*, November 13, 2024, https://www.scmp.com/tech/tech-trends/article/3286276/chinas-hottest-ai-bot-bytedances-doubao-tops-charts-51-million-active-users
16. Smartphone maker insights, February 11, 2025, https://www.idc.com/promo/smartphone-market-share/market-share/
17. Global smartphone market grew by a modest 0.2% in Q1 2025, despite regional declines, *Canalys*, April 30, 2025, https://canalys.com/newsroom/worldwide-smartphone-market-q1-2025

18. Mainland China's smartphone market grew 5% in Q1 2025, Xiaomi returned to top after decade, *Canalys*, April 27, 2025, https://canalys.com/newsroom/china-smartphone-market-q1-2025
19. Gregory C. Allen, In chip race, China gives Huawei the steering wheel, Center for Strategic and International Studies, October 6, 2023, https://www.csis.org/analysis/chip-race-china-gives-huawei-steering-wheel-huaweis-new-smartphone-and-future
20. Evelyn Cheng, Chinese smartphone maker releases a new operating system, *CNBC*, October 27, 2023, https://www.cnbc.com/2023/10/27/chinese-smartphone-company-xiaomi-releases-hyperos-as-it-plans-car.html
21. Ben Thompson, Xiaomi's Ambition, *Stratechery*, January 7, 2015, https://stratechery.com/2015/xiaomis-ambition/
22. Rebecca A. Fannin, *Tech Titans of China*, Nicholas Brealey, 2019, https://www.amazon.com/Tech-Titans-China-challenging-innovating-ebook/dp/B07MJ5Y7B4
23. Wang Xing, Bloomberg Billionaires Index, #294, https://www.bloomberg.com/billionaires/profiles/xing-wang/

Chapter 4

1. Eleanor Olcott, US tech sector pressures Chinese venture capital to divest, *Financial Times*, June 7, 2024, https://www.ft.com/content/4fb99b07-159f-4539-8e50-e85d66c585e6
2. Wave of departures, *Asia Business Law Journal*, December 11, 2024, https://law.asia/why-us-law-firms-leave-china/
3. *National Venture Capital Association 2025 Yearbook*, March 27, 2025, https://nvca.org/2025-yearbook/
4. Tim Siccion, Neel Hiteshbhai Bharucha, China, India private equity deals plunge in 2024 as exits jump, *S&P Global*, January 22, 2025, https://www.spglobal.com/market-intelligence/en/news-insights/articles/2025/1/china-india-private-equity-deals-plunge-in-2024-as-exits-jump-86848684
5. Thilo Hanemann, Armand Meyer, and Danielle Goh, *Vanishing Act: The Shrinking Footprint of Chinese Companies in the US*, Rhodium Group, September 7, 2023, https://rhg.com/research/vanishing-act-the-shrinking-footprint-of-chinese-companies-in-the-us/
6. Harriett Agnew plus five reporters, China pulls back from US private equity investments, *Financial Times*, April 21, 2025, https://www.ft.com/content/478c1c64-8923-4ec2-858d-670b30ae44f9
7. EY releases the overview of China outbound investment of 2024, *EY Greater China*, February 13, 2025, https://www.ey.com/en_cn/newsroom/2025/02/ey-releases-the-overview-of-china-outbound-investment-of-2024

8. Insights, M&A highlights, *Mergermarket*, December 18, 2024, https://ionanalytics.com/insights/dealogic/ecm-highlights-fy24/
9. 2024 IPO wrapped, EY Global IPO Trends 2024, December 18, 2024, https://www.ey.com/en_gl/newsroom/2024/12/2024-ipo-wrapped-americas-and-emeia-recover-asia-pacific-lags
10. Jon Bateman with foreword by Eric Schmidt, *US–China Technological Decoupling*, Carnegie Endowment for International Peace, April 25, 2022, https://carnegieendowment.org/research/2022/04/us-china-technological-decoupling-a-strategy-and-policy-framework?lang=en
11. Ibid.
12. Ardi Janjeva, Seoin Baek, and Andy Sellars, *China's Quest for Semiconductor Self-Sufficiency*, Center for Emerging Technology and Security, Alan Turing Institute, December 4, 2024, https://cetas.turing.ac.uk/publications/chinas-quest-semiconductor-self-sufficiency
13. Robert Atkinson, China is rapidly becoming a leading innovator in advanced industries, *Information Technology & Innovation Foundation*, September 2024, https://www2.itif.org/2024-chinese-innovation-exec-sum.pdf
14. The four key strengths of China's economy, *Harvard Business Review*, August 26, 2024, https://hbr.org/2024/08/the-4-key-strengths-of-chinas-economy-and-what-they-mean-for-multinational-companies
15. Evelyn Cheng, U.S. regulatory scrutiny fans Chinese stock delisting fears, *CNBC's The China Connection Newsletter*, April 23, 2025, https://www.cnbc.com/2025/04/23/cnbc-the-china-connection-newsletter-chinese-stocks-risk-us-delisting.html
16. Muslim Farooque, Goldman Sachs warns of $800B US sell-off in worst-case China split, *Yahoo Finance*, April 17, 2025, https://finance.yahoo.com/news/goldman-sachs-warns-800b-u-150246042.html
17. Chinese Companies Listed on Major US Exchanges, China Securities Regulatory Commission, March 7, 2025, https://www.uscc.gov/research/chinese-companies-listed-major-us-stock-exchanges
18. US-Listed China Internet Stocks: fact vs. fiction, *CNBC*, April 21, 2025, https://www.cnbc.com/2025/04/23/cnbc-the-china-connection-newsletter-chinese-stocks-risk-us-delisting.html
19. Sun Yu and Cheng Leng, China puts brakes on US stock listings for homegrown companies, *Financial Times*, February 27, 2025, https://www.ft.com/content/a5640320-7ed3-47c5-b9a1-2c0d600170be
20. See Rebecca A. Fannin, *Tech Titans of China*, 1st edn, John Murray Press, 2019, ch. 2, Tables 2.3–2.5.
21. Kia Kokalitcheva, TikTok resolution may use Grindr's path as precedent, *Axios*, April 27, 2024, https://www.axios.com/2024/04/27/biden-tiktok-sale-grindr

Chapter 5

1. Alex Konrad, The Midas List 2024, *Forbes*, June 4, 2024, https://www.forbes.com/lists/midas/
2. Emily Weinstein and Ngor Luong, U.S. outbound investment into Chinese AI companies, February 2023, https://cset.georgetown.edu/publication/u-s-outbound-investment-into-chinese-ai-companies
3. Summary of Select Committee investigation findings on American venture capital fueling the PRC military and human rights abuses, Venture Capital Report Summary, February 8, 2024, https://selectcommitteeontheccp.house.gov/sites/evo-subsites/selectcommitteeontheccp.house.gov/files/evo-media-document/2.8.24%20SCC%20Venture%20Capital%20Report%20Summary.pdf
4. Ibid.
5. Select Committee launches investigations into U.S. venture capital firms funding problematic PRC companies, press release, July 19, 2023, https://selectcommitteeontheccp.house.gov/media/press-releases/select-committee-launches-investigations-us-venture-capital-firms-funding
6. Tabby Kinder and George Hammond, Intel venture arm's China tech stakes raise alarm in Washington, *Financial Times*, July 16, 2024, https://www.ft.com/content/0217cab2-c9a3-4ffa-993a-39874d6d803f
7. The Select Committee on the CCP; Letters, Letter to Sequoia Capital, October 17, 2023, https://selectcommitteeontheccp.house.gov/media/letters/letter-sequoia-capital-its-prc-high-tech-investments-examine-implications-announced
8. The CCP's Investors, How American Venture Capital Fuels the PRC Military and Human Rights Abuses, February 8, 2024; https://selectcommitteeontheccp.house.gov/sites/evo-subsites/selectcommitteeontheccp.house.gov/files/evo-media-document/2024-02-08%20-%20VC%20Report%20-%20FINAL.pdf
9. ByteDance board members, https://www.bytedance.com/en/
10. The CCP's investors: how American venture capital fuels the PRC military and human rights abuses, The Select Committee on the Strategic Competition between the US and the Communist Party, February 8, 2024, https://selectcommitteeontheccp.house.gov/sites/evo-subsites/selectcommitteeontheccp.house.gov/files/evo-media-document/2024-02-08%20-%20VC%20Report%20-%20FINAL.pdf
11. Rebecca Feng, A year ago, a star banker was detained in China, *The Wall Street Journal*, February 2, 2024, https://www.wsj.com/business/a-top-chinese-banker-who-was-detained-last-year-has-resigned-62b88ac3

12. Adam Lysenko, Testimony before the US–China Economic and Security Review Commission, March 19, 2021, https://www.uscc.gov/annual-reports
13. Data provided by private equity research firm Preqin in London.
14. Joyce Guervarra, US-backed funding rounds in China fall to lowest level in a decade, S&P Global, June 6, 2024, https://www.spglobal.com/market-intelligence/en/news-insights/articles/2024/6/us-backed-funding-rounds-in-china-fall-to-lowest-in-a-decade-81822765
15. Camille Boullenois, Endeavour Tian, and Laura Gormle, The mountain is high, the lead investor is far away, September 11, 2024, Rhodium Group, https://rhg.com/research/the-mountain-is-high-the-lead-investor-is-far-away/
16. Karen Gilchrist, US pension funds heavily invested in China tech, December 12, 2023, https://www.cnbc.com/2023/12/12/us-pension-funds-heavily-invested-in-china-despite-crackdown.html
17. Yifan Wei, Yuen Yuen Ang, and Nan Jia, The promise and pitfalls of government guidance funds in China, *The China Quarterly* 256 (2023): 939–59, https://www.cambridge.org/core/journals/china-quarterly/article/promise-and-pitfalls-of-government-guidance-funds-in-china/9211F2954E797A29E82B540DA6D9A714
18. The Complete List of Unicorn Companies, *CB Insights*, January 2025, https://www.cbinsights.com/research-unicorn-companies
19. The Crunchbase Unicorn Board, *Crunchbase*, June 6, 2025, https://news.crunchbase.com/unicorn-company-list/#:~:text=Table_title:%20$5.9%20trillion%20Table_content:%20header:%20|%20Company,Money%20Value:%20$66B%20|%20Country:%20China%20|
20. Eleanor Olcott and Wang Xueqiao, How China has throttled its private sector, *Financial Times*, September 12, 2024, https://www.ft.com/content/1e9e7544-974c-4662-a901-d30c4ab56eb7
21. Meaghan Tobin, *New York Times*, June 25, 2024, https://www.nytimes.com/2024/06/25/business/china-ipo-initial-public-offer.html; Chinese companies listed on major US stock exchanges, US–China Economic and Security Review Commission, March 7, 2025, https://www.uscc.gov/research/chinese-companies-listed-major-us-stock-exchanges
22. 2024 review and 2025 outlook for Chinese Mainland & HK IPO markets, *Deloitte*, December 19, 2024, https://www2.deloitte.com/cn/en/pages/audit/articles/2024-review-and-2025-outlook-for-chinese-mainland-and-hk-ipo-markets.html
23. Jeff Diehl, 2025 Global investor survey, Adams Street, March 21, 2025, https://www.adamsstreetpartners.com/insights/2025-global-investor-survey/

24. Chinese startups suffers as IPOs freeze, Reuters, November 24, 2024, https://www.reuters.com/markets/asia/chinese-startups-suffer-ipo-freeze-prompts-investors-exercise-redemption-rights-2024-11-25/
25. Eleanor Olcott and Wang Xueqiao, How has China throttled its private sector, *Financial Times*, September 12, 2024, https://www.ft.com/content/1e9e7544-974c-4662-a901-d30c4ab56eb7
26. Robert Wu, CEO, BigOne Lab, *LinkedIn*, April 16, 2024, https://www.linkedin.com/posts/robert-wu-03778a19b_chinas-venture-capital-industry-is-dying-activity-7186309254826373120-ky6G/
27. Research institute Merics (Mercator Institute for China Studies), https://merics.org/en/report/accelerator-state-how-china-fosters-little-giant-companies
28. Scott Kennedy and Qin Mei, Two years in, how does the STAR market measure up? *CSIS*, January 24, 2022, https://www.csis.org/blogs/trustee-china-hand/two-years-how-does-star-market-measure
29. Tabby Kinder and Eleanor Olcott, Sequoia Capital's former China unit raises new $2.5bn start-up fund, *Financial Times*, July 8, 2024, https://www.ft.com/content/4a31e233-a649-4a09-b708-30f99e4ce99e
30. Rita Liao, GGV split off China business, *TechCrunch*, September 21, 2023, https://techcrunch.com/2023/09/21/ggv-splits-off-china-business-following-congressional-panel-probe/
31. The CCP's investors: how American venture capital fuels the PRC military and human rights abuses, The Select Committee on the Strategic Competition between the US and the Communist Party, February 8, 2024, https://selectcommitteeontheccp.house.gov/sites/evo-subsites/selectcommitteeontheccp.house.gov/files/evo-media-document/2024-02-08%20-%20VC%20Report%20-%20FINAL.pdf
32. Rita Liao, GGV split off China business, *TechCrunch*, September 21, 2023, https://techcrunch.com/2023/09/21/ggv-splits-off-china-business-following-congressional-panel-probe/
33. Brent Crane, All In, *The Wire China*, January 19, 2025, https://www.thewirechina.com/2025/01/19/all-in-kai-fu-lee-ai/
34. Qiming Venture Partners completes fundraising of RMB 6.5 billion, *Qiming News*, May 18, 2023, https://www.qimingvc.com/cn/news/20230518-QM-cn

Chapter 6

1. Explosive report on Chinese AI firm DeepSeek, press release, April 16, 2025, https://selectcommitteeontheccp.house.gov/media/press-releases/moolenaar-krishnamoorthi-unveil-explosive-report-chinese-ai-firm-deepseek
2. Forget FAANG, CNBC video, May 30, 2025, https://www.cnbc.com/video/2025/05/30/kristina-shen-jack-altman-ai.html
3. Ken Yeung, The prompt, *The AI Economy*, June 6, 2025, https://theaiecon-omy.substack.com/p/mary-meeker-10-charts-that-define-the-ai-boom
4. Kai-Fu Lee, *AI Superpowers*, Houghton Mifflin Harcourt, 2018.
5. Robert D. Atkinson, China is rapidly becoming a leading innovator in advanced industries, Information Technology & Innovation Foundation, September 16, 2024, https://itif.org/publications/2024/09/16/china-is-rapidly-becoming-a-leading-innovator-in-advanced-industries/
6. Hodan Omaar, China's AI unicorns: five startups vying rival Western counterparts, Information Technology & Innovation Foundation, December 12, 2024; https://itif.org/publications/2024/12/12/chinas-ai-unicorns-five-startups-vying-rival-western-counterparts/
7. How to access Chinese LLMs, *MIT Technology Review*, March 24, 2025, https://www.facebook.com/technologyreview/posts/hundreds-of-chi-nese-large-language-models-have-been-released-since-the-governmen/1020915083230975/
8. Juro Osawa and Qianer Liu, DeepSeek, a national treasure in China, is now being closely guarded, *The Information*, March 14, 2025, https://www.theinformation.com/articles/deepseek-national-treasure-china-now-closely-guarded
9. Emily Weinstein and Ngor Luong, US outbound investment in Chinese AI companies, Center for Security and Emerging Technology, February 2023, https://cset.georgetown.edu/wp-content/uploads/CSET-U.S.-Outbound-Investment-into-Chinese-AI-Companies.pdf
10. Kyle Wiggers, OpenAI calls DeepSeek state-controlled, *TechCrunch*, March 13, 2025, https://techcrunch.com/2025/03/13/openai-calls-deep-seek-state-controlled-calls-for-bans-on-prc-produced-models/
11. DeepSeek on government devices, The Conference Board Newsletters and Policy Alerts, March 21, 2025, https://www.conference-board.org/research/CED-Newsletters-Alerts/state-and-federal-governments-deepseak-ban
12. 2024 IPO Wrapped, EY Global IPO Trends 2024, December 18, 2024, https://www.ey.com/en_gl/newsroom/2024/12/2024-ipo-wrapped-americas-and-emeia-recover-asia-pacific-lags

13. The 2025 AI Index at Stanford HAI reports US private AI investment grew to $109.1 billion—nearly 12 times China's $9.3 billion. GenAI saw particularly strong momentum, attracting $33.9 billion globally in private investment—an 18.7 percent increase from 2023. https://hai.stanford.edu/ai-index/2025-ai-index-report
14. Gene Teare, *Crunchbase News*, January 7, 2025, https://news.crunchbase.com/venture/global-funding-data-analysis-ai-eoy-2024/
15. State of AI Report: 6 trends shaping the landscape in 2025, January 30, 2025, https://www.cbinsights.com/research/report/ai-trends-2024/
16. Hodan Omaar, China's AI unicorns: exploring the five startups vying to rival Western Counterparts, Information Technology & Innovation Foundation, December 12, 2024, https://itif.org/publications/2024/12/12/chinas-ai-unicorns-five-startups-vying-rival-western-counterparts/
17. Chris Menko, Eye on AI, *Crunchbase News*, January 23, 2025, https://news.crunchbase.com/ai/most-active-investors-2024-a16z-databricks-xai/
18. Chris Metinko, Will DeepSeek burst VC's AI bubble? *Crunchbase*, January 27, 2025, https://news.crunchbase.com/ai/chinas-deepseek-tech-openai-nvda/
19. Artificial Intelligence Market, *Fortune Business Insights*, May 5, 2025, https://www.fortunebusinessinsights.com/industry-reports/artificial-intelligence-market-100114
20. Paul Mozur and Cade Metz, In one key A.I. metric. China pulls ahead of the U.S.: talent, *New York Times*, March 22, 2024, https://www.nytimes.com/2024/03/22/technology/china-ai-talent.html
21. Hodan Omaar, How innovation is China in AI? Information Technology & Innovation Foundation, August 26, 2024, https://itif.org/publications/2024/08/26/how-innovative-is-china-in-ai/
22. *Patent Landscape Report—Generative Artificial Intelligence*, WIPO 2024, https://www.wipo.int/web-publications/patent-landscape-report-generative-artificial-intelligence-genai/en/index.html
23. Tripp Mickle, Apple's AI ambitions for China provoke Washington's resistance, *New York Times*, May 17, 2025, https://www.nytimes.com/2025/05/17/technology/apple-alibaba-ai-tool-china.html
24. Hao Nan, Opinion: China's AI push in the Global South is not just about technology, *South China Morning Post*, March 2, 2025, https://www.scmp.com/opinion/china-opinion/article/3300271/chinas-ai-push-global-south-not-just-about-technology
25. Select Committee on the Strategic Competition between the United States and the Chinese Communist Party, American VC firms investing billions into PRC companies fueling the CCP's military, surveillance

state, and Uyghur genocide, February 8, 2024, https://selectcommitteeontheccp.house.gov/media/press-releases/committee-report-american-vc-firms-investing-billions-prc-companies-fueling

26. Kimberly Cao, Baidu launches new reasoning AI model in challenge to DeepSeek, *The Wall Street Journal*, March 16, 2025, https://www.wsj.com/tech/ai/baidu-launches-new-reasoning-ai-model-in-challenge-to-deepseek-2778af6e
27. Dylan Butts, Alibaba launches open-source AI model, *CNBC*, March 26, 2025, https://www.cnbc.com/2025/03/27/alibaba-launches-open-source-ai-model-for-cost-effective-ai-agents.html
28. Dylan Butts, China's open-source embrace upends conventional wisdom around artificial intelligence, *CNBC*, March 27, 2025, https://www.cnbc.com/2025/03/27/alibaba-launches-open-source-ai-model-for-cost-effective-ai-agents.html
29. Ibid.
30. Coco Feng, Tencent's Hunyuan T1 AI reasoning model rivals DeepSeek, *South China Morning Post*, March 22, 2025, https://www.scmp.com/tech/big-tech/article/3303456/tencents-hunyuan-t1-ai-reasoning-model-rivals-deepseek-performance-and-price
31. Tencent joins AI spending race, *Reuters*, March 19, 2025, https://www.reuters.com/technology/tencent-joins-chinas-ai-spending-race-with-2025-capex-boost-2025-03-19/
32. Mike Wheatley, ByteDance sets aside about $20B for AI spending this year, *Silicon Angle*, January 23, 2025; https://siliconangle.com/2025/01/23/report bytedance-sets-aside-around-20b-ai-spending-year/
33. ByteDance plans $25 billion capex in 2025, *Reuters*, January 23, 2025, https://www.reuters.com/technology/bytedance-plans-20-billion-capex-2025-mostly-ai-sources-say-2025-01-23/
34. Tomas Casas and Guido Cozzi, *Elite Quality Report 2025: The Sustainable Value Creation of Nations*, May 6, 2025, https://papers.ssrn.com/sol3/papers.cfm?abstract_id=5241721
35. Hodan Omaar, How innovative is China in AI?, Information Technology & Innovation Foundation, https://itif.org/publications/2024/08/26/how-innovative-is-china-in-ai/
36. Raffaele Huang, One of America's hottest entertainment apps is Chinese-owned, *The Wall Street Journal*, July 27, 2024, https://www.wsj.com/tech/ai/one-of-americas-hottest-entertainment-apps-is-chinese-owned-04257355
37. Saritha Rai and Yoolim Lee, China AI startup stockpiled 18 months of Nvidia chips before ban, *Bloomberg*, November 9, 2023, https://www.bloomberg.com/news/articles/2023-11-10/china-ai-startup-stockpiled-18-months-of-nvidia-chips-before-ban

Chapter 7

1. Charlie Campbell, The trouble with sharing, *Time*, April 2, 2018, https://time.com/5218323/china-bicycles-sharing-economy/
2. Ibid.
3. Michelle Toh, *CNN Business*, December 29, 2017, https://money.cnn.com/2017/12/29/investing/china-bike-sharing-boom-bust/
4. Rebecca Fannin, Crash of China bike-sharing startup Ofo costs leading VCs big-time, *Forbes*, March 8, 2019, https://www.forbes.com/sites/rebeccafannin/2019/03/08/crash-of-china-bike-sharing-startup-ofo-costs-leading-vcs-big-time/
5. Beatrice LaForga, IWG takes over last Ucommune space in Hong Kong, *Mingtiandi*, July 18, 2023, https://www.mingtiandi.com/real-estate/flexible-office/iwg-takes-over-last-ucommune-space-in-hong-kong-as-four-centres-open/; WSJ Markets, Ucommune International, financials, https://www.wsj.com/market-data/quotes/UK/financials
6. Silicon Drago Shanghai 2017, September 13, 2017, https://www.silicondragonventures.com/news/silicon-dragon-shanghai-2017-highlights/
7. Ellen Huet, WeWork Sells Control of China Business in $200 Million Deal, *Bloomberg*, September 23, 2020, https://www.bloomberg.com/news/articles/2020-09-23/wework-sells-control-of-china-business-in-200-million-deal
8. https://www.wework.cn/en-US/what-is-wework/
9. Chris Udemans, China tech investor: DiDi's evolving saga, *TechNode*, July 30, 2021, https://technode.com/2021/07/30/china-tech-investor-didis-evolving-saga-and-beijings-regulatory-ambitions-with-kendra-schaefer/=
10. Song Jingli, DiDi says its English interface platform serves 2 million users in China over 2 years, *KrAsia*, September 24, 2019, https://kr-asia.com/didi-says-its-english-interface-platform-served-2-million-users-in-china-over-2-years
11. Ride-Hailing—China, *Statista*, https://www.statista.com/outlook/mmo/shared-mobility/ride-hailing/china
12. Catherine Clifford, 30 most valuable venture-backed companies in the world, *CNBC*, May 15, 2024, https://www.cnbc.com/2018/05/15/pitchbook-30-most-valuable-venture-backed-companies-in-the-world.html
13. Omar Manky and Natalia Mogollón, How DiDi Chuxing adapts to Latin America's era of digital platforms, *Carnegie Europe*, July 1, 2024, https://carnegieendowment.org/research/2024/07/how-didi-chuxing-adapts-to-latin-americas-era-of-digital-platforms?center=europe&lang=en

14. Vishakha Saxena, China's DiDi tried to defraud investors with 2021 IPO: US Court, *Asia Financial*, March 15, 2024, https://www.asiafinancial.com/chinas-didi-tried-to-defraud-investors-with-2021-ipo-us-court
15. Chinese ride-hailing company DiDi must face US investor lawsuit, *CNBC / Reuters*, March 15, 2024, https://www.cnbc.com/2024/03/15/chinese-ride-hailing-company-didi-global-must-face-us-investor-lawsuit-over-ipo.html
16. Jill Shen, China's DiDi sets new target for ride-hailing as crackdown ends: report, *TechNode*, October 10, 2023, https://technode.com/2023/10/10/chinas-didi-sets-new-target-for-ride-hailing-as-crackdown-ends-report/
17. Wenyi Zhang, Number of cars per 100 households, 2009 and 2023, *Statista*, https://www.statista.com/statistics/278432/privately-owned-passenger-cars-in-china/
18. Vinod Sreeharsha and Mike Isaac, Didi Chuxing, China's Ride-Hailing Giant, Agrees to Buy Uber Rival in Brazil, *The New York Times,* January 3, 2018; https://www.nytimes.com/2018/01/03/technology/didi-chuxing-99-brazil-ride-hailing.html
19. DiDi announces results for fourth quarter and full year 2023, March 23, 2024, https://s28.q4cdn.com/896456191/files/doc_financials/2023/q4/DiDi_2023_Q4_Press_Release_.pdf; United States Securities Exchange Commission, Form 20-F 2023, https://d18rn0p25nwr6d.cloudfront.net/CIK-0001764757/0e449f11-49b1-4815-bb8b-32efd3300d58.pdf
20. China ride-hailing firm DiDi says Q4 revenue rises 7.1% as demand recovers after crackdown, *Reuters*, March 18, 2025; https://tech.yahoo.com/business/articles/didi-reports-7-1-revenue-091319200.html
21. Omar Manky and Natalia Mogollón, How DiDi Chuxing adapts to Latin America's era of digital platforms, Carnegie's Political Economy Initiative, July 1, 2024, https://carnegieendowment.org/research/2024/07/how-didi-chuxing-adapts-to-latin-americas-era-of-digital-platforms?lang=en¢er=middle-east

Chapter 8

1. Michael Bush, Chinese E-commerce giants want your business—US retailers are losing it, *MarketWatch*, August 21, 2024, https://www.marketwatch.com/story/chinese-e-commerce-giants-want-your-business-and-u-s-retailers-are-losing-it-314e096f
2. Louise Matsakis, How Temu and Shein snuck up on Amazon, *Big Technology* podcast, May 29, 2024, https://www.linkedin.com/pulse/how-shein-temu-snuck-up-amazon-alex-kantrowitz-v7xke/

3. Zijing Wu and Laura Onita, Shein explores US restructuring as tariffs threaten to derail London IPO, *Financial Times*, April 30, 2025, https://www.ft.com/content/37b30f64-f9e8-4c1a-ad50-23e7c61880a7
4. Dylan Butts, Temu and Shein face massive tariffs, *CNBC*, May 6, 2025,https://www.cnbc.com/2025/05/06/temu-shein-face-big-us-tariffs-dont-count-them-out-experts-say.html
5. Annie Palmer, Temu halts shipping direct from China, *CNBC*, May 2, 2025, https://www.cnbc.com/2025/02/02/trump-tariffs-take-aim-at-trade-loophole-used-by-temu-shein.html
6. Shein, Temu and Chinese E-commerce, US–China Economic and Security Commission, April 14, 2023, https://www.uscc.gov/research/shein-temu-and-chinese-e-commerce-data-risks-sourcing-violations-and-trade-loopholes
7. Select Committee releases interim findings from Shein & Temu forced labor investigation, June 22, 2023, https://selectcommitteeontheccp.house.gov/media/press-releases/select-committee-releases-interim-findings-shein-temu-forced-labor
8. Diane Rinaldo, Looking beyond TikTok: the risks of Temu, *CSIS*, October 24, 2024, https://www.csis.org/analysis/looking-beyond-tiktok-risks-temu
9. Temu shoppers are loyal, pretty social, Retail Customer Experience, October 7, 2024; Temu and Shein conceding US market share, *Marketplace Pulse*, April 24, 2025, https://www.marketplacepulse.com/articles/temu-and-shein-conceding-us-market-share
10. Retail Customer Experience.com, Temu shoppers are loyal, pretty social, October 7, 2024, https://www.retailcustomerexperience.com/news/temu-shoppers-are-loyal-pretty-social/
11. Annie Palmer, Amazon debuts discount store with everything under $20 to take on Temu and Shein, *CNBC*, November 13, 2024, https://www.cnbc.com/2024/11/13/amazon-haul-discount-storefront-debuts-to-take-on-temu-and-shein-.html
12. Brian Delp, Are Amazon and WalMart competing in a losing race with Shein and Temu? *LinkedIn Pulse*, August 20, 2024, https://www.linkedin.com/pulse/amazon-walmart-competing-losing-race-shein-temu-brian-delp-c54qe/
13. International Trade Administration, https://www.trade.gov/country-commercial-guides/china-ecommerce
14. Quarterly retail e-commerce sales, February 19, 2025, https://www.census.gov/retail/ecommerce.html#:~:text=Total%20e%2Dcommerce%20sales%20for,15.3%20percent%20of%20total%20sales

15. Charlene Liu, China E-commerce, HSBC Research, March 11, 2024, https://www.gbm.hsbc.com/en-gb/insights/global-research/china-ecommerce; Penetration rate of online shopping in China from 2014 to 2024, *Statista*, https://www.statista.com/statistics/302071/china-penetration-rate-of-online-shopping/
16. F. Watty, Online shopping behavior in the United States - statistics & facts, *Statista*, March 10, 2025, https://www.statista.com/topics/2477/online-shopping-behavior/
17. Casey Hall, How Temu's China owner PDD stacks up against Alibaba and JD.com, *Reuters*, September 2, 2024,https://www.reuters.com/business/retail-consumer/how-does-pdd-stack-up-against-other-big-china-e-ecommerce-firms-2024-08-30/
18. Alibaba Group, DBS Treasures, February 21, 2025, https://www.dbs.com.hk/treasures/aics/stock-coverage/templatedata/article/equity/data/en/DBSV/012014/9988_HK.xml
19. Rachel Treisman, What to know about RedNote, the Chinese app that American TikTokkers are flooding, *NPR*, January 17, 2025, https://www.npr.org/2025/01/15/nx-s1-5260742/tiktok-china-rednote-xiaohongshu-app
20. Chinese social media Xiaohongshu moves closer to IPO as profits surge in 2024, sources say, *South China Morning Post*, December 13, 2024, https://sg.finance.yahoo.com/news/chinese-social-media-xiaohongxu-moves-093000430.html
21. Charlie Campbell, How China is cracking down on its once untouchable tech titans, *Time*, May 20, 2021, https://time.com/6048539/china-tech-giants-regulations/
22. Eustance Huang, Analyst argues that China's regulation of Ant Group is bad for financial technology, *CNBC*, December 29, 2020, https://www.cnbc.com/2020/12/30/regulation-of-ant-group-is-bad-for-china-economy-fintech-analyst.html
23. Alizila staff, Alibaba's core businesses reignite growth as ai strategy delivers strong results, *Alizila*, February 20, 2025, https://www.alizila.com/alibabas-core-businesses-reignite-growth-as-ai-strategy-delivers-strong-results/

Chapter 9

1. Tesla Motors in China, Silicon Dragon Shanghai 2014, *YouTube*, September 18, 2014, https://www.youtube.com/watch?v=beWECu42nlI

2. Anniek Bao, Tesla posted record China sales in 2024, *CNBC*, January 6, 2025, https://www.cnbc.com/2025/01/06/tesla-china-sales-2025-as-competition-heats-up-.html; China's BYD cuts entry price for smart EVs to below $10,000, *Reuters*, February 10, 2025, https://www.reuters.com/business/autos-transportation/chinas-byd-sell-21-models-with-its-gods-eye-smart-driving-tech-2025-02-10/
3. Andrei Nedelea, Strong performance in China defied 2024 global sales downturn, *InsideEVs*, January 4, 2025, https://insideevs.com/news/746181/tesla-china-sales-increased-2024/
4. Kristin Toussaint, 'I don't want to give it up': Ford CEO Jim Farley has been driving a Chinese EV for months, *Fast Company*, October 24, 2024, https://www.fastcompany.com/91216063/i-dont-want-to-give-it-up-ford-ceo-jim-farley-has-been-driving-a-chinese-ev-for-months
5. Global EV Outlook, International Energy Agency, May 14, 2025, https://www.iea.org/reports/global-ev-outlook-2025/executive-summary
6. Suvrat Kothari, Shenzhen, City of superchargers, *InsideEVs*, May 8, 2024, https://insideevs.com/news/718971/shenzen-city-of-superchargers-ev-stations-surpass-gas/
7. Rui Ma, Factory tourism having a moment, *LinkedIn*, May 9, 2025, https://www.linkedin.com/feed/
8. Evaluation of the parking and maneuvering capabilities of the BYD YangWang U7 2025, AI & Car, *YouTube*, April 20, 2025, https://www.youtube.com/watch?v=lP7MqEcQczc
9. Michael Dunne, Driving the future of U.S.–China relations: China's global automotive push, *Asia Society*, February 27, 2019, https://asiasociety.org/video/driving-future-us-china-relations-chinas-global-automotive-push
10. Victor Tangermann, Tesla forced to change name of full self-driving in China, *Futurism*, March 26, 2025, https://futurism.com/tesla-change-name-full-self-driving-china
11. KrAsia Connection, Tesla forced to suspend China FSD trial under stricter update rules, *KrAsia*, March 24, 2025, https://kr-asia.com/tesla-forced-to-suspend-china-fsd-trial-under-stricter-update-rules
12. Andrew Hawkins, Tesla reportedly launches FSD in China—or has it?, *The Verge*, February 25, 2025, https://www.theverge.com/news/619092/tesla-fsd-china-update-falls-short
13. Daniel Ren and Yujie Xue, Sci-fi to reality: Chinese EV makers outpace Tesla in the autonomous-driving race, *SCMP*, March 29, 2025, https://www.scmp.com/business/china-evs/article/3304267/sci-fi-reality-chinese-ev-makers-outpace-tesla-autonomous-driving-race

14. Keith Bradsher, China is testing more driverless cars than any other country, *New York Times*, June 13, 2024, https://www.nytimes.com/2024/06/13/business/china-driverless-cars.html
15. Abhijeet Kumar, Elon Musk reveals robotaxi: Will Tesla face the same challenges as China?, *Business Standard*, October 11, 2024, https://www.business-standard.com/world-news/elon-musk-reveals-robotaxi-will-tesla-face-the-same-challenges-as-china-124101100373_1.html

Chapter 10

1. Seth Kurkowski, Every DJI drone is out of stock on the company's online store, *DroneDJ*, June 23, 2025, https://dronedj.com/2025/06/23/every-dji-drone-is-out-of-stock-on-the-companys-online-store/
2. US Sanctions US drone maker DJI, *BBC*, December 17, 2021, https://www.bbc.com/news/technology-59703521
3. Ibid.
4. Miriam McNabb, Commerce Department issues NPRM to limit use of Chinese-made drones and components, *Drone Life*, January 3, 2025, https://dronelife.com/2025/01/03/commerce-department-issues-nprm-to-limit-use-of-chinese-made-drones-and-components/
5. Effects of interior's policies on foreign-made drones, US Government Accountability Office, September 25, 2024, https://www.gao.gov/products/gao-24-106924
6. DJI Media Center, DJI creates high-security solution for government drone programs, June 24, 2019, https://www.dji.com/newsroom/news/dji-creates-high-security-solution-for-government-drone-programs
7. Sean Hollister, DJI says US Customs is blocking its drone imports, *Verge*, October 16, 2024, https://www.theverge.com/2024/10/16/24272188/dji-blames-us-customs-block-import-some-drones
8. Drone Market Size & Trends, Grand View Research, Forecast Period, 2025–2030, https://www.grandviewresearch.com/industry-analysis/drone-market-report
9. China's new drone mothership, *New York Post*, May 19, 2025, https://nypost.com/2025/05/19/world-news/chinas-new-drone-mothership-draws-online-ridicule-big-slow-and-not-stealthy/
10. The Top 29 Drone Companies in 2025, *DroneU*, December 9, 2024, https://www.thedroneu.com/blog/top-drone-companies/
11. Rebecca A. Fannin, *Tech Titans of China*, 1st edn, John Murray Press, 2019, ch. 10, The Age of Drones and Robots.
12. DJI Innovations IPO, *Linqto*, https://www.linqto.com/ipo/dji-innovations/

13. Kate Kelly, A Chinese drone is America's favorite drone maker, except in Washington, *New York Times*, April 25, 2024, https://www.nytimes.com/2024/04/25/us/politics/us-china-drones-dji.html
14. World Robotics 2024 presentation, International Federation of Robotics, September 24, 2024, https://ifr.org/ifr-press-releases/news/record-of-4-million-robots-working-in-factories-worldwide
15. Yorko Kubota and Raffaele Huang, Man versus machine, *The Wall Street Journal*, April 19, 2025, https://www.wsj.com/tech/man-versus-machine-as-china-shows-off-humanoid-robots-in-half-marathon-75d7e766
16. International Federation of Robotics, September 24, 2024, https://ifr.org/downloads/press2018/Press_Conference_2024.pdf
17. Caiwei Chen, China's EV giants are betting big on humanoid robots, *MIT Technology Review*, February 14, 2025, https://www.technologyreview.com/2025/02/14/1111920/chinas-electric-vehicle-giants-pivot-humanoid-robots/
18. Taylor Herzlich, Elon Musk's Optimus humanoid robots steal show at Tesla, *New York Post*, October 11, 2024, https://nypost.com/2024/10/11/business/elon-musks-optimus-humanoid-robots-steal-show-at-tesla-event-this-will-be-the-biggest-product-ever/
19. Yi Luo, AI to reshape the world, Alibaba founder Jack Ma, *South China Morning Post*, January 9, 2025, https://www.scmp.com/tech/tech-trends/article/3294054/ai-set-reshape-world-alibaba-founder-jack-ma-tells-chinese-rural-teachers
20. Kurt Knutsson, China's newest humanoid robot ready to serve like never before, *Fox News*, January 11, 2025, https://www.foxnews.com/tech/chinas-newest-humanoid-robot-ready-serve-like-never-before
21. Jacqueline Du, The global market for humanoid robots could reach $38 billion, Goldman Sachs, February 27, 2024, https://www.goldmansachs.com/insights/articles/the-global-market-for-robots-could-reach-38-billion-by-2035
22. Could AI robots help fill the labor gap? Morgan Stanley Research, August 13, 2024, https://www.morganstanley.com/ideas/humanoid-robot-market-outlook-2024#:~:text=Morgan%20Stanley%20analysts%20estimate%20that,roughly%20%243%20trillion%20in%20payroll
23. Robert Atkinson, How innovative is China in the robotics industry?, Information Technology & Innovation Foundation, March 11, 2024, https://itif.org/publications/2024/03/11/how-innovative-is-china-in-the-robotics-industry/
24. Jacqueline Du, The global market for humanoid robots could reach $38 billion, *Goldman Sachs*, February 27, 2024, https://www.

goldmansachs.com/insights/articles/the-global-market-for-robots-could-reach-38-billion-by-2035

25. Robert Atkinson, How innovative is China in the robotics industry?, Information Technology & Innovation Foundation, March 11, 2024, https://itif.org/publications/2024/03/11/how-innovative-is-china-in-the-robotics-industry/
26. Ibid.
27. The Humanoid 100: mapping the humanoid robot value chain, Morgan Stanley Research, February 6, 2025, https://advisor.morganstanley.com/john.howard/documents/field/j/jo/john-howard/The_Humanoid_100_-_Mapping_the_Humanoid_Robot_Value_Chain.pdf
28. Yuanyue Dang, China Says Humanoid Robots Are New Engine of Growth, *South China Morning Post*, November 3, 2023, https://www.scmp.com/news/china/politics/article/3240259/china-says-humanoid-robots-are-new-engine-growth-pushes-mass-production-2025-and-world-leadership
29. Jacqueline Du, The global market for humanoid robots could reach $38 billion, *Goldman Sachs*, February 27, 2024, https://www.goldmansachs.com/insights/articles/the-global-market-for-robots-could-reach-38-billion-by-2035
30. Thomas Barrabi, Chinese-made humanoid robots raise alarms in Congress, *New York Post*, August 5, 2024, https://nypost.com/2024/08/05/business/chinese-made-humanoid-robots-raise-alarms-in-congress-stealth-army-on-our-land/; Katie Britt and Jacob Helberg, Humanoid robots are the next threat from China, *WSJ Opinion*, September 26, 2024,https://www.wsj.com/opinion/humanoid-robots-are-the-next-threat-from-china-e0c88a26
31. Robert Atkinson, How Innovative is China in the Robotics Industry?, Information Technology & Innovation Foundation, March 11, 2024, https://itif.org/publications/2024/03/11/how-innovative-is-china-in-the-robotics-industry/
32. Digital Drift TV, TikTok video, February 26, 2025, https://www.tiktok.com/@digitaldrifttv/video/7465452769151929633

Chapter 11

1. Scott Cohn, Wisconsin wants to be tech mecca, *CNBC*, https://www.cnbc.com/2024/06/25/wisconsin-wants-to-be-tech-mecca-and-leave-the-foxconn-fail-behind.html

Index